Democracy
and
American
Foreign
Policy

A Foreign Policy Research Institute Book

This book is part of a series of works sponsored by the
Foreign Policy Research Institute in Philadelphia.
Founded in 1955, the Institute is an independent, nonprofit
organization devoted to research on issues affecting
the interests of the United States.

Democracy and American Foreign Policy

Reflections on the Legacy of Alexis de Tocqueville

ROBERT STRAUSZ-HUPÉ

Transaction Publishers
New Brunswick (USA) and London (UK)

Copyright © 1995 by Transaction Publishers, New Brunswick, New Jersey 08903

All rights reserved under International and Pan-American Copyright Conventions. No part of this book may be reproduced or transmitted in any form or by any means, electronic or mechanical, including photocopy, recording, or any information storage and retrieval system, without prior permission in writing from the publisher. All inquiries should be addressed to Transaction Publishers, Rutgers—The State University, New Brunswick, New Jersey 08903.

Library of Congress Catalog Number: 94-9585
ISBN: 1-56000-175-5 (cloth)
Printed in the United States of America

Library of Congress Cataloging-in-Publication Data

Strausz-Hupé, 1903–
     Democracy and American foreign policy :   reflections on the legacy of Alexis de Tocqueville / Robert Strausz-Hupé ; with a foreword by Walter A. McDougall
        p. cm.
     Includes bibliographical references and index.
     ISBN 1-56000-175-5 (cloth)
     1. United States—Foreign relations—1989- —Philosophy. 2. Tocqueville, Alexis de, 1805-1859—Influence. I. Title.
E840.S78   1994
327.73—dc20   94-9585
                                                                  CIP

*Democratic institutions awaken and foster
a passion for equality which they can never
satisfy.*

*In the principle of equality I discern two
tendencies: the one leading the mind of every
man to untried thoughts; the other prohibit-
ing him from thinking at all.*

*If ever the free institutions of America are
destroyed, that event may be attributed to the
unlimited authority of the majority.*

—Alexis de Tocqueville

Contents

Part IV

Part V

Foreword

Strausz-Hupé's Foresight

Walter A. McDougall

> Marxian analysis has been left behind.... But this does not explain the failure of the Soviet Union—and fail it did.
>
> The Soviets still can veto the making of a new world order; they can no longer create it.
>
> The United States...has not a coherent vision of the future, its own and that of mankind.
>
> The American spirit is that of an open society—open to all men and all cultures—and the political genius of America is the federative idea.
>
> The coming world order will mark the last phase in a[n] historical transition and cap the revolutionary epoch of this century.

The preceding quotations could, could they not, be snippets of presidential speeches, scholarly articles, or op-ed pieces dating from 1989 to 1991? Instead, they appeared in a remarkable article published thirty-five years ago in the premier issue of *Orbis*. That was when Robert Strausz-Hupé, University of Pennsylvania professor and a founding father of that peculiarly American discipline of "international relations,"[1] implicitly dedicated the Foreign Policy Research Institute to the quest for what his article called a *novus orbis terrarum*—a new world order—hence, the title of the journal.[2]

Strausz-Hupé, born in Kaiser Franz Josef's Vienna in 1903, has lived a half dozen lives: as a Wall Street broker, freelance writer and lecturer,

---

Walter A. McDougall is the Alloy-Ansin Professor of International Relations at the University of Pennsylvania and editor of *Orbis*. This foreword originally appeared in the Winter 1992 issue of *Orbis*.

wartime combatter of Nazi propaganda, professor and intellectual impresario, ambassador, advisor to presidents, and prolific apologist for American policy throughout the cold war. This last role made him a *bête noir* of the University of Pennsylvania's anti-Vietnam War movement, and his image among subsequent generations of students became that of a hawkish realist who supposedly incriminated his university by association with so-called American militarism. A few earnest activists may have tried to understand Strausz-Hupé, for instance by reading his autobiography, *In My Time* (Norton, 1965). But that seems doubtful: the book has been checked out of the University of Pennsylvania library just five times since 1969. More to the point, young Americans, as Strausz-Hupé observed, had a hard time imagining the inhuman nature of totalitarianism, whose abiding threat gave rise to the cold war and—rightly or wrongly—to the Vietnam War. Hence the irony—and the challenge—in the fact that, if there was to be a new world order, it was up to the otherwise innocent Americans to will it, design it, and sacrifice to bring it about. "It is in the nature of the historical process that the debris of decaying institutions serves as fertilizer for the growth of the future order."[3] But the seeds must be sowed by the United States.

The Era of Revolution

Strausz-Hupé named his inaugural *Orbis* article, "The Balance of Tomorrow," after his Ph.D. thesis written in the closing days of World War II,[4] and it adumbrates the conclusions he had drawn as of age fifty-three. He began by defining the era since 1914 as revolutionary, by which he meant an era when "the bottom layers of the political universe have been set in motion," one permanent structure after another crumbles away, and "each solemn compact, hailed as a return to order, is overtaken and rescinded by events" (page 10). This was hardly controversial—Henry Kissinger was at that moment drawing a similar comparison to the French Revolutionary era in his dissertation.[5]

Nor was Strausz-Hupé unique in noting that the twentieth century's revolutionary swings were magnified and accelerated by science and technology. It was a commonplace of the atomic age that history was speeding up, and that science had outpaced man's ability to manage it and himself. But Strausz-Hupé illustrated the point with a startling summary of the reversals of alliances that marked the era of the world wars, reversals that gave the lie to any ideological consistency on the part of the Great Powers, whose "principles and practices appear to trip drunkenly over one another" (page 12). Only "the ingenious services of the mass media, conjuring up an orderliness and rationality where there are none" (page 13) had reconciled the American people to their own government's lurches from neutrality to crusade in 1917; from crusade to aloofness, then isolation, after World War I; from isolation to interventionism and alliance—even with the Soviet Union—in 1941; and from cooperation with the Soviets to hostility towards Moscow and alliance with Germany and Japan. Clearly such policies were the products of prudence rather than principle, and if there was meaning in the fantastic storms of the century, it was not in the desperate tacking of stricken ships of state, but in the storm itself, in the process.

The United States and World Federalism

"The issue before the United States is the unification of the globe under its leadership within this generation" (page 14). Unification of the globe was the only solution to the two threats hanging over humanity: not the USSR (whose collapse Strausz-Hupé already foresaw in 1956, while others thought its power cresting), but rather the demographic and political explosion of Asia on the one hand, and nuclear proliferation on the other. The United States had to take the lead in forging a new world order because it was the only power capable of doing so, and because the Americans' federative genius suited them to the task. And it had to be done soon, because the survival of the United States, of Western culture, and possibly of mankind depended on it.

This was the necessary outcome of the revolution of the twentieth century. Anarchy could not be allowed to continue, but in a revolutionary era, the old multipolar balance-of-power system—the nineteenth-century model—could not be resurrected. It had rested, at least until 1890, on Christian and/or secular liberal values and a self-restraint common to all the European great powers. Those prerequisites no longer existed. Hence the only alternative to global anarchy was unity among the Western powers, and then among all the powers on the face of the globe.

So it would seem that Strausz-Hupé, *soi-disant* reactionary, was in fact an apostle of world federalism. Perhaps it is not surprising, given

his roots in the multinational Habsburg monarchy. To him, the nation-
state was an odious invention of French ideology, "restrained neither by
liberal constitutions nor by concern for the common interests of mankind," and hence "the greatest retrogressive force of this century" (page
17). The story of the twentieth century was that of the struggle of what
he called the "federative power" to replace nationalism as the organiz-
ing principle of world politics. Seen in this light, the Nazi Third Reich
and the Japanese Co-Prosperity Sphere had been stabs, albeit horribly
flawed, at supranational organization. All they proved, however, was
that "the nation state cannot transcend itself" (page 18). Soviet communism made a more credible appeal to supranational unity, but in practice
it betrayed its economic promises, exploited its allies, and conjured "the
genii of Asian nationalism to do the work of communism" (page 19).
Strausz-Hupé predicted, just a few years before the Sino-Soviet split,
that the USSR would regret this ploy.

That left the United States "the one and only truly revolutionary power
of this century" (page 19). Alone among the great powers, the United
States was future-oriented, composed of many nations, open to limitless
assimilation, tolerant, generous, humanist, and pragmatic—all the things
Soviet communism was not. Americans were also economic revolution-
aries dedicated to free enterprise, free trade, new technology, and interdependence. All that made the United States a candidate for global
leadership.

Moreover, the United States alone possessed the requisite federative
power, derived from its de facto control of the Western hemisphere and
the Pacific, its NATO partnership with Western Europe, and its leadership in the United Nations. Strausz-Hupé had no illusions about the last.
He thought the United Nations a weak reed, to be replaced someday by
new institutions of American design. The most important source of federative power was NATO, destined to be "the nucleus of the world fed-
eration-in-the-making" (page 23). The European states, in order to correct
the current imbalance of power between them and the United States,
would have to unite. The resulting voluntary American-European union
could then confront with confidence the hostile Asian masses until such
time as Asia stabilized and begged to cooperate. At the same time, the
wealth and "sheer decency of the American scheme for universal partnership will inexorably persuade the Soviet masses (who, too, aspire to

a middle class status) across the heads of the communist bosses to defect to freedom" (page 24).

One can imagine what foreign or leftist critics would have to say of all this: world federation was a fig leaf for hegemony, for an American empire or Pax Americana. And so it was, wrote Strausz-Hupé. A new world order must be "the American universal empire" to the extent that it bore America's stamp. But it was more than that: "The mission of the American people is to bury the nation states, lead their bereaved peoples into larger unions, and overawe with its might the would-be saboteurs of the new order who have nothing to offer mankind but a putrifying ideology and brute force" (page 26). He gave the United States fifty years—until 2007—to accomplish the task, by which time its energies might be exhausted. But if it succeeded, he foresaw an American empire that was just another name for mankind, and whose fruits were universal order, peace, and happiness.

Objections to Federalism

Of course, objections leap to mind, starting with Strausz-Hupé's concept of the revolutionary age dating from 1914, and ending . . . now? A structuralist, celebrating the stability of cold war bipolarity, might consider that 1989 marked the beginning, not the end, of a revolutionary era. And how can Strausz-Hupé suggest that Nazi and Japanese imperialism had a federative quality without impugning the reputation of his own, benign project? Whatever internationalism informed German and Japanese policy was a function of the needs of their racist war machines, a fact that Strausz-Hupé exposed to great effect at the time.[6] Furthermore, he expected Europeans to unite in order to escape American (or Russian) domination, then turn around and join a federation that the author grants is a sort of "American empire." Why would they do that? Is American federative power truly strong enough—and manifestly benign enough—to dominate the world without provoking resistance from erstwhile enemies and friends alike? Is the maintenance of sovereignty and the balance of power not the first law of nature in the realists' view of international politics? In any case, if the effort of containing Russians and Asians and of building a new world order will likely exhaust the United States, as Strausz-Hupé predicted, how can the order be maintained once it is set up? In 1956, American federative power—military, economic, and moral—was indeed immense. In 1991, it is not; Paul Kennedy had a point.[7] The military burden carried by Americans for the past thirty-five years, the private and public profligacy that has emptied America's treasury and sapped its savings, and the current deficits, lack of competitiveness, cultural confusion, and self-doubt exhibited by the United States all suggest that its federative power is severely diminished. At the same time, American pragmatism, dedication to free enterprise and trade, and technological dynamism are not in evidence as they once were. Finally, the security imperative that undergirded the Atlantic Alliance seems to be shrinking as the cold war withers away. It would seem that world federalism becomes possible only when it is no longer so necessary, and that, in any case, the United States is no longer in a position to foot the bill for it.

Thus, the issue of whether the end of the cold war will lead to a new world order comes to depend less on the United States and more on the federative powers latent in Europe, the USSR (or whatever replaces it), and Japan. Perhaps the historical role of the United States was not to forge an American empire after all, but rather to hold the fort against totalitarianism until such time as the revived victims and perpetrators of Nazi, Japanese, and Soviet imperialism themselves embraced the federalist solution. Nor is that scenario as inconceivable as a tough-minded realist might think. If the G-7 states (Britain, Canada, France, Germany, Italy, Japan, and the United States), augmented by a reformed Soviet Union, set themselves the task of coordinating their economic, security, and environmental policies along the same lines as Europe 1992—and if the East European states and someday even the USSR joined NATO—then a new world order might emerge in just the way Strausz-Hupé envisioned thirty-five years ago. What it would mean is that Western Civilization—or, to use the most ancient term, Christendom—would regain its unity after not one, but five centuries of intramural warfare, the epoch of the "rivalry of the Great Powers." From San Francisco around the northern hemisphere to Vladivostok, a league of nations might emerge that embraces common notions of law and human rights based on the secularized Judaeo-Christian imagination, that shares common political and economic institutions, and that commands power and pelf sufficient to intimidate and in time attract the peoples of China, Hindustan, Araby, and Africa.[8] (To be sure, Japan is a wild card in this otherwise

well-ordered deck, and one that Strausz-Hupé did not need to empha-
size in 1957. But if we assume the permanence of liberal parliamentarism
in Japan, and Japan's continued need for access to Western markets,
then it is hard to imagine Tokyo opting out of a new world order.)

But the question remains, as it does inside the European Community
today, what exactly does federalism mean? What would, or should, a
new world order be like? And how is it coming about? The ear catches
echoes of Hegelianism in Strausz-Hupé's "process-history" leading inexorably through balance of power politics to global unity,[9] and antici-
pations of Francis Fukuyama's "end of history" in Strausz-Hupé's
predicted triumph of liberal democracy.[10] Is Strausz-Hupé a Central
European historicist, or an American empiricist? Does his world federalism stem from Kant, in whose imagination federalism must inevitably
emerge from power politics and self-interest, or from Woodrow Wilson,
who imagined the nations spurning power politics for an idealistic regime of international law?

Echoes of Kant

Kant began his own thinking on global federalism with Rousseau's
definition of an international state of nature as "a state of war which
constantly threatens if it is not actually in progress"—Hobbes writ large.
Nothing in this state of affairs would lead automatically to unity and
peace. Rather, "the state of peace must be *founded*."[11] But no state, Kant
held, would voluntarily relinquish its sovereignty, or entrust its security,
to a supranational body in the manner of citizens within a state. Hence,
the "universal republic" of the philosophers was a chimera. The new
world order must be a *Volkerbund* (federation of nations) rather than a
Volkerstaat (supranational state). The theoreticians of the old Holy Roman Empire, the living model of federalism, likewise endorsed a
Staatenbund (federation of states) over a *Bundestaat* (single federal state).

Moreover, the federal entity must, if it is to survive, make its member
states more secure than they would be on their own, and strengthen,
rather than weaken, their autonomy. In other words, an international
union is possible only if candidate governments calculate that they would
have less control over their fates outside the union than inside it. This
was Kant's great insight, and it made his scheme for "perpetual peace"
realistic rather than utopian. At the base of his conception lay the "cos-

mopolitan or world law," which banned the absorption of one state by another or interference by force in the internal affairs of other states, and enjoined all parties to practice "universal hospitality"—free right of passage and commerce (though not of immigration) for foreigners.

How, in Kant's view, would this happy state of affairs come about? First, it would not happen through world government or through the imposition of a hegemonic empire, but through voluntary treaties—*foederes*—which is what he meant by the word "federal." Secondly, it would occur only after a lengthy learning process punctuated by ever more terrible wars. Thus, "what appears to be complicated and accidental in individuals may yet be understood as steady, progressive, though slow, evolution of the original endowments of the entire species.... All the natural faculties of a creature are destined to unfold themselves completely and according to an end." Nature (or Nature's God) thus imparts meaning to history, and patterns and progress exist, even if they are barely discernible to the men and states who trace them out. For men are not animals acting on dumb instinct, but they nevertheless have to learn to employ their reason as Nature intended. Only "many devastations, reversals, and a very general exhaustion of the states' resources, may accomplish what reason could have suggested to them without so much sad experience, namely: to leave the lawless state of savages and to enter into a union of states."[12] And Kant, writing at the time of the French Revolution, believed the day of reason not too distant, if only because "the periods in which equal progress is achieved will become shorter and shorter."[13] History, in other words, was speeding up.

In all of Strausz-Hupé's books, one encounters only two brief references to Kant, one involving Kant's political geography, the other in connection to Heidegger's philosophy. (As for Hegel, he was part of Strausz-Hupé's discarded intellectual baggage: "In my attic molders the luggage of German philosophy, including the valise marked Schopenhauer and Hegel."[14]) How then did he reach conclusions that parallel so strikingly Kant's vision of what federalism means, and how it is to come about?

The Cold War Roots of World Federalism

Federalism was part of the currency of the European resistance movement during World War II, but Strausz-Hupé apparently came to it along a quite different path. The Nazi geopolitician Andreas Haushofer be-

lieved that the struggle among races for space and power must end ultimately in a world empire. Strausz-Hupé suspected that he was right, but
of course rejected the conclusion that a Nazi-dominated "heartland empire" was the inevitable winner.

Strausz-Hupé's first allusion to a new world order appeared in *Geopolitics* (1942). In that work, he foresaw that modern technology and
global economic integration were changing the relationship of geography to society and must "drive men's thoughts about the world's political organization into yet untried channels."[15] The models he found for a
new organization—this is in 1942, mind you—were in Lend-Lease and
the Atlantic Charter, which symbolized "the mission of the United States
in this age: to put an end to the era of rampant expansionism.... No
matter what world order arises from the present struggle...[i]t is in the
interest of the United States no less than in that of humanity that there
should be one nucleus from which a balancing and stabilizing control,
the power of arbiter, be exercised...the United States."[16] Haushofer
himself identified the Americans as the only existing people possessing
the geographical prerequisites for global land, sea, and air power; hence,
they were the real arch-enemy of pan-Germanism. All the Americans
lacked (unlike the Nazis) was a *Weltanschauung*—a "pan-idea"—to
undergird an imperialist thrust outside their own hemisphere.[17] Strausz-
Hupé, building on Franklin Roosevelt's liberal internationalism, sought
to provide that "pan-idea."

After World War II, mankind faced a choice among three futures:
endless geopolitical conflict, a world hegemony, or a world federation.
The third, wrote Strausz-Hupé, was the "American solution"[18]—but "the
proceedings in San Francisco" that founded the United Nations were
not the answer. Even if the new superpowers—the United States, the
Soviet Union, and the British Empire—remained friendly, they could
never concert their action against any countries other than the defeated
fascist states, for the reason that the rest of the world already lay within
the sphere of influence of one or another of the victorious powers.[19]
Thus, as soon as the United Nations tried to manage affairs anywhere
but in Germany or Japan, it would turn into an instrument of coercion
and threat against one of the very powers on which it depended for its
existence.

By 1952, in the midst of the Korean War, this fact was manifest; the
Soviets clung to their alternative notion of a new world order, and geopolitics resumed its tyranny over the affairs of mankind. The world was

split, even the West was divided, and federalism seemed as far off as ever. But by then—and here is the essence of his originality—Strausz-Hupé saw in the struggle against Sovietism the mechanism by which his vision might yet take form. Not in the United Nations, not in peaceful coexistence, not in the convergence of East and West (a notion he rejected as early as 1945), but, rather, in the institutions of the cold war itself lay the foundation for the emerging global federalism. The Marshall Plan and NATO were not the utopian creations of abstract philosophy, but pragmatic, contingent responses to the ongoing geopolitical competition with the Soviet-dominated Eurasian heartland. (Strausz-Hupé saw at once the paradox that the West combatted Marxism in Europe with the materialistic weapons of economics and arms, while the materialist Soviets continued to act on the allegedly bourgeois belief that ideas, conspiracies, and charisma can move mountains. The paradox deepened in the 1960s when religiously motivated conservatives took to defending capitalism with such materialist arguments as "It outperforms communism," while so-called scientific Marxists had little choice but to attack capitalism with moral arguments.)

So the decisive issue was this: if the West were to survive, it had to remain whole, for the Soviets and the Chinese could profit strategically only by exploiting the divisions among their enemies. But it was by no means certain that the Western peoples could summon the will to hang together, for they had lost the necessary faith in their own culture. Thus, the political crisis was also a spiritual crisis. "I was raised in the Protestant faith," wrote Strausz-Hupé. "Of its theological teachings I kept little."[20] And yet he described, in language similar to Max Weber's, Whittaker Chambers's, or Daniel Bell's, the disenchantment and resulting demoralization that afflicted Western civilization coincident with the rise of scientific-technological mass society. Cut off from the roots of their own notions of right and wrong and of the purpose of life, Europeans and Americans were prey to materialism and anomie. Communism was "the religion of the antichrist in the most literal sense, precisely because it drew its message from the Scriptures and denied the source upon which it had fed. Not to see this is to fall into the trap historical materialism has set for reason."[21] In effect, Strausz-Hupé was asking why men should take risks for freedom and a better world unless they love truth, justice, peace, and decency as much as their lives and comfort; and why they should love those things unless they held fast to a faith immanent in the products of their own culture, a faith that "does move mountains."[22] Western survival and world order demanded an integrative impulse, a zeal for those things that bind men together, and hence a rejection of the "disintegrative ideologies" peddled by the patrons of race and class warfare, and of the "zone of indifference" inhabited by European existentialists.

So the world's fulcrum rested, in the 1950s, on the spirit of the American people, on whether they cared, or succumbed to a selfishness that could not, in the long run, save even themselves. "If a new culture, a world culture, should arise, Anglo-Saxondom may be the golden bridge across which the old culture will join the new."[23] Thanks to their openness to foreign immigrants, ideas, and goods, Americans were the only possible architects of an empire-without-imperialism. It was at this point in 1952 that Strausz-Hupé sketched the blueprint he would announce five years later in the first issue of *Orbis*. First, Western Europe must unite, for a "Europe that is mere object cannot cooperate."[24] But European integration could not occur if the old continent's energies were drained into military spending. Hence the United States itself must deter the USSR until Europe fully recovered, reconciled its working classes, and developed "new, supranational loyalties."

Once this was achieved, the Soviet bloc would stand in relief as a "clumsy and backward despotism" and the East Europeans would feel an "irresistible pull." In time, the Soviets would have to accept a negotiated settlement including the evacuation of its armies and the reunification of Germany.[25] The West would then again be whole, and provide a framework into which the rest of the world, in the fullness of time, would ask to be fitted. To be sure, it would be a long, arduous process; every step must be taken, and in proper order. But if the West found the will to do so, it would also forge, serendipitously, the engine of global unity. For "the defense of freedom is thus a fraternal, a federative enterprise. That enterprise confers justice and nobility upon the uses of power."[26]

Recent Developments

Since those words were written, NATO has faced a long series of crises, each labelled terminal at the time, and survived. The European Community has been born, and has deepened and broadened to the point that it now contemplates political union. East Europeans have persevered through numerous heartbreaks to break free finally of Moscow and petition for membership in the EC and NATO. Germany has reunified and is fully lodged in the European and Atlantic communities. The U.S.-Japanese alliance has survived bitter controversy, and no prudent person in either country contemplates jettisoning the partnership, however much they may seek its re-adjustment. The Soviet Union has liberalized, shrugged off a neo-Stalinist coup, and will in all likelihood ask to join the Western-led economic community. Thus, much of what Strausz-Hupé envisioned has come to pass, thanks to the federative power mediated through the institutions born of the cold war. He even predicted that the Chinese would remain aloof, the last to join the world.

It remains to be seen whether all this will eventuate in a new world order that amounts to a federalist *Staatenbund*. Kant's stricture probably still applies: states will join only insofar as their autonomy is enhanced, not inhibited, by membership. Elites may see that this is so, that to remain outside the new world order is to condemn oneself to impotence over forces that will profoundly affect one's own country. But can the masses be reconciled to the apparent management of domestic affairs by foreigners? Can nationalism, born in the lifetime of Kant and seemingly an atavism in Strausz-Hupé's view, be contained, or will what John Lewis Gaddis calls the forces of fragmentation cancel out the forces of integration?[27] The collapse of Yugoslavia and the apparently chaotic disassembly of the Soviet Union would seem to bode ill. But we must also respect the irony of the fact that ethnic consciousness, even inter-ethnic hostility, played a positive role in the revolt against the false federalism of socialist internationalism. Moreover, the nationalistic impulses of the smaller East European peoples, by themselves, are not sufficient to do more than delay the federative process, however vexing they may be. The future of that part of the world depends, rather, on whether "reason" (as Kant had it) has succeeded in educating Germans and Russians about the wisdom of federative institutions.

On a more metaphysical plane one may ask—ironically, given Strausz-Hupé's earlier fears—whether the political victory of the West may be cancelled out by its ongoing spiritual retreat. Democracy and free enterprise seem triumphant, but the question remains: what are peace and freedom for? The core of Western civilization today is emptier now than it was in the 1950s. Is the new world order just a way to make the world safe for nihilism, hedonism, and self-worship—a community for the purpose of evading community? Will the whole world, even the Muslims, someday enter into the Zone of Indifference, and mankind quench its fires, only to perish from ice?

Notes

1. Stanley Hoffman, "An American Social Science: International Relations," *Daedalus,* Summer 1977, pp. 41–60.
2. Robert Strausz-Hupé, "The Balance of Tomorrow," *Orbis,* April 1957, pp. 10–27. All parenthetical page numbers refer to this article.
3. Robert Strausz-Hupé and Stefan T. Possony, *International Relations in the Age of Conflict between Democracy and Dictatorship* (New York: McGraw Hill, 1954), p. 807.
4. Robert Strausz-Hupé, *The Balance of Tomorrow: Power and Foreign Policy in the United States* (New York: G.P. Putnam's Sons, 1945).
5. Henry A. Kissinger, *A World Restored: The Politics of Conservatism in a Revolutionary Age* (Boston, Mass.: Houghton Mifflin, 1957).
6. See Robert Strausz-Hupé, *Axis America: Hitler Plans Our Future* (New York: G.P. Putnam's Sons, 1941), and *Geopolitics: The Struggle for Space and Power* (New York: G.P. Putnam's Sons, 1942).
7. Paul Kennedy, *The Rise and Fall of the Great Powers* (New York: Random House, 1987).
8. See Walter A. McDougall, "Speculations on the Geopolitics of the Gorbachev Era," in Alfred J. Rieber and Alvin Z. Rubinstein, eds., *Perestroika at the Crossroads* (Armonk, N.Y.: M.E. Sharpe, 1991), pp. 326–62.
9. See, for instance, the Hegelian/Rankean Ludwig Dehio, *The Precarious Balance: Four Centuries of the European Power Struggle* (New York: Alfred A. Knopf, 1962), originally published as *Gleichgewicht oder Hegemonie* (Crefeld: Sherpe Verlag, 1948), who predicted that postwar bipolarity must inevitably give way to a universal empire—and better an American empire than a Russian one.
10. Francis Fukuyama, "The End of History?" *The National Interest,* Summer 1989, pp. 3–18.
11. Immanuel Kant, *Thoughts on Perpetual Peace* (1795), quoted by F.H. Hinsley, *Power and the Pursuit of Peace* (New York: Cambridge University Press, 1967), p. 62. See also C.J. Friedrich, *Inevitable Peace* (Cambridge, Mass.: Harvard University Press, 1948).
12. Hinsley, *Power and the Pursuit of Peace,* pp. 74–75.
13. Ibid., p. 80.
14. Robert Strausz-Hupé, *In My Time* (New York: W.W. Norton, 1965), p. 33.
15. Strausz-Hupé, *Geopolitics,* p. 193.
16. Ibid., p. 195.
17. Ibid., pp. 65–67.
18. Strausz-Hupé, *The Balance of Tomorrow,* p. 276.
19. Ibid., pp. 30–38.

20. Strausz-Hupé, *In My Time*, p. 278.
21. Robert Strausz-Hupé, *The Zone of Indifference* (New York: G.P. Putnam's Sons, 1952), p. 73. Also published as *The Estrangement of Western Man* (London: Gollancz, 1953).
22. Ibid., p. 60.
23. Ibid., p. 76.
24. Ibid., p. 288.
25. Ibid., pp. 288–99.
26. Robert Strausz-Hupé, *Power and Community* (New York: Praeger, 1956), p. 128.
27. John Lewis Gaddis, "Toward the Post-Cold War World," *Foreign Affairs,* Spring 1991, pp. 102–22.

Author's Preface

I came to America, like Alexis de Tocqueville, to observe American democracy at work, and, having seen, to return to Europe, enriched by my American experience, to make a place for myself in one of the democratic countries of Europe. Also like Tocqueville, I had my doubts about the possibility of uniting liberty and equality. But, unlike Tocqueville, I eventually came to still my doubts. Tocqueville returned to France, taking with him his admiration of American democracy as well his skepticism. I stayed.

From what I had seen, I concluded that The Good Society would confound its enemies, at home and abroad, and would prevail over the forces of conformity and anarchy that were threatening to engulf European society. Not all of my doubts about the efficacy of democratic government have been stilled, particularly in the field of foreign affairs. However, I now consider democracy's failings a challenge rather than an irremediable deficiency.

To take but one instance, which I discuss below: I believe the most disabling impediment to the making of America's foreign policy has been its inordinate subservience to domestic politics, and, hence, to factions. In chapter 12, I examine how one powerful lobby has succeeded for many years in having the United States pursue the lobby's policy rather than the policy consistently recommended by presidents of both parties, notwithstanding the Constitution's clear intention of vesting the executive with the power of determining America's foreign relations.

But I do not see that lobbies of such awesome power are inherent in a democratic system. And, I would note, the United States has done remarkably well in achieving international success despite the clash of conflicting claims: between the executive and legislative powers, between the government and the lobbies, and amongst the lobbies themselves. The costs of this arrangement have been enormous, but, though scandalously wasteful, it has worked: the United States is the most powerful country in the world, and whatever peace there is on this earth is due to the exertions of its flawed and paradoxical system.

Will things stay this way? Only if we see that they do.

In this book, I argue that the overarching purpose of American diplomacy must be the defense of democracy everywhere, and, hence, the universalization of democracy. "To make the world safe for democracy." Let us not be afraid to say it.

Obviously, this purpose clashes with the isolationism and hedonism of the American people. So too does the necessary instrument of foreign policy—a diplomatic elite—clash with American populism. But the relevant questions are not whether we need a foreign policy—we do—or whether foreign policy should be in the hands of a professional elite—it should. The relevant questions are: How can a diplomatic elite make foreign policy in full view of the people, and execute it in compliance with a popular mandate, when that mandate is ever-changing and always tending towards isolationism?

These are difficult questions for American democracy at any time, but they are of special urgency today. The United States now confronts international issues as pressing and ominous as those that, for the last fifty years, faced American statesmanship. The cold war may have ended; but the demographical revolution is about to begin. Ever larger populations are pressing upon the land. Technology and science are more creative than they have ever been; but the destructiveness of their creations is more terrifying than it has ever been, and more widely available. The world has gotten smaller and more vulnerable. The system of nation states is failing on all counts: ecology, trade, public safety, and physical as well as mental health.

Since these phenomena are worldwide, they must be dealt with internationally. Yet the United States must take the lead in confronting them. Indeed, only the United States can take the lead. The question is: Will it?

I wager on an the undisputed characteristics of the American people: their team spirit. Americans are at their best when called upon to do great things together. In this century, they have shown that they can set aside their isolationism and hedonism and band together with other free peoples in a defense against anarchy and tyranny.

In my final chapter, I will argue that free peoples now must band together permanently; that the historic state system—the system of national sovereignties—has become unworkable; and that the essential solution to the problems facing the world is easily stated: a new political order, a federation of the democracies.

For the generous support that made this book possible, I would like to thank the Foreign Policy Research Institute, the Heritage Foundation, the United States Institute of Peace, and the Earhart Foundation.

Introduction

Ever since the First World War, the crucial question that has confronted the United States is the defense of Western civilization. It will remain so for at least another two generations of Americans.

I assume that the defense of Western civilization is in the national interest of the United States, if only because American democracy is inconceivable in any other context. I shall not attempt to prove the proposition.

The question that I shall seek to answer here is only this: Can the American people agree upon and consistently pursue foreign policies that serve this national interest which their democracy has in defending Western civilization? To answer this question, I will examine certain popular and often paradoxical American attitudes towards society and the state, politics and government, the instruments of foreign affairs and the people who wield them.

To examine those attitudes, I begin by turning to Alexis de Tocqueville, as any sensible person must.

Equality, Democracy, and Liberty

When Alexis de Tocqueville came to America, more than half a century had elapsed since the Republic's successful bid for independence and more than forty years since the making of its Constitution. Most Americans had been born into the Republic. If they gave the matter any thought, they considered themselves to be its free and equal citizens. Put into today's clinical language, Americans had found their identity.

Tocqueville's *Democracy in America* documents these momentous events—the creation of a distinct polity like no other. As a historical document, felicitously crafted at a time of universal social ferment and systemic crisis, the book has no equal. With regard to the United States, Tocqueville got it right, and that is why his *Democracy* is still being read

1

as a concise introduction to the social and political history of early America.

Of infinitely greater importance, however, Tocqueville got it right with regard to democracy. And that is why his book is still being read as a gloss on the idea of democracy as such, an idea that knows no national borders. It is being read as an essay in political philosophy that addresses the abiding danger of popular government, to wit, the danger that liberty will be destroyed by a passion for equality, the passion that is, ironically, also the originating fount of liberty.

In *The Persians* of Aeschylus, when the Queen of the Persians is told of her navy's defeat, she asks who rules over the victorious Greeks and is taken aback by the answer: "They are the servants of no man and no man's subject."[1] Ever since ancient Greece, the claim to freedom has rested on the claim of equality—whether equality of social position (as in Aristotle's *Politics*) or equality before God (as in Thomas Jefferson's *Declaration of Independence*). On the understanding that no equal, or group of equals, may dictate a person's life, this equality becomes the foundation both of government derived from the people and of individual liberty. In America, Alexis de Tocqueville found the conjunction between the two pursued further than it had ever been.

Yet Tocqueville came to doubt—not that equality and liberty could be united—for in America they obviously had—but that American democracy would be able to resist the pull of equality. He foresaw, accurately, that egalitarianism would lead the country to vote itself into a paternalistic state, all the more absolute for being benevolent and having been freely chosen by the people.

Leadership and Foresight

For the purposes of this book, with its focus on foreign policy, the chief paradox perhaps is that democratic peoples call for leadership but are loathe to submit to the discipline leadership entails. They want leadership as well as an equality of condition that cannot be reconciled with the hierarchical nature of leadership. They want leaders who are forceful and respected, yet chummily egalitarian, and who, thus, must pretend to be what they are not. It is from these strands of contradiction that American democracy seeks to weave a consensus in foreign policy, one that will withstand the trials of civil strife, economic crisis, and war.

The democratic peoples want a quick return on their investment in good government, such as no good government can provide, since all great undertakings require time, often measured in generations rather than years. Yet, the term of presidential office is only four years and of a seat in the House of Representatives, only two. The mark of statesmanship is the ability to foresee, but the democratic peoples require statesmen to follow policies that will be appealing at the next election—despite all partisanship can say, true or false, against them.

History takes time. Two full generations were needed to validate the policy of containment; nine presidents, and more than twenty Congresses, participated in carrying it out, with highly varying degrees of enthusiasm. It seems that the vast changes and challenges ahead of this and following generations of democratic statesmen call for far-reaching Constitutional amendments.

The alternative to Constitutional change is—luck: the good luck that America will have political leaders who put country ahead of their taste for power. Some do. During the Gulf crisis, President George Bush, reading the graphs of public opinion and mindful of the Vietnam syndrome, could not fail to conclude that, by going to war against Iraq, rather than relying on economic sanctions, he was putting his re-election at risk.[2] That these counsels did not shake the president's resolution suffices to confirm the oldest and amply documented axiom of statesmanship: to qualify one needs strong nerves and strong convictions. The president, as the opposition has not cared to controvert, had both. The outcome was due to his sagacity and courage. For the country, it meant victory. For the president, it meant defeat.

The Future of History

Today, an air of gratified finality appears to hover over America's foreign policy establishment. The cold war is over. The time has come to shrink the structures that were built to fight it. The economic collapse of the Soviet Union, though fraught with many uncertainties (some quite ominous), opens vast opportunities, political and economic. The threat of war in Europe has receded. In the Middle East, the Soviet Union (and, later, the Russian Republic) cooperated with the United States in the liberation of Kuwait from Saddam Hussein's Iraq, for many years the USSR's most important Arab client.

Upon the collapse of the Soviet Union and the dissolution of the Warsaw Pact, the administration's assessment of the Soviet threat changed
enough to warrant a sizable reduction of the U.S. armed forces, the can-
cellation of arms acquisitions contracted for by the Reagan administration, and the acceleration of negotiations of arms control treaties. Leaving
aside the question how well the U.S. national security will be served by
these treaties and other treaties yet still in the drafting stage, one fact is
beyond dispute: the great majority of Americans is well pleased with the
administration's policies of arms reduction and rapprochement with the
Commonwealth of Independent States.

So, the tenor of the great debate about U.S. foreign policy has shifted,
even as the balance of power has shifted. In place of the two superpowers, there is only one. And there will be only one into the foreseeable
future, for only the United States can bear the burden of being a superpower.

Since the United States is prepared to, or, in any event, compelled to
play this role, all assumptions about the distribution of world power
need to be reviewed. A new order must rise from the dissolution of the
old. The question is not whether it will, but what it will be like.

Notes

1. "They are slaves to none, nor are they subject." Aeschylus, "The Persians," act 1,
scene 1, line 232, trans. by S.G. Benardete, in *Aeschylus Two; Four Tragedies*,
ed. David Grene and Richmond Lattimore (Chicago, Ill.: University of Chicago
Press, 1969).
2. Said the respected *Economist* (December 1, 1990, p. 23): "A recent poll in the
Los Angeles Times made Mr Bush's troubles plain. Since August, support for the
course he has charted has fallen from 75% to just above 50%; it took Lyndon
Johnson three years, and hundreds of body bags, to drop as far. Only 42% of
respondents supported (compared with 52% who opposed) the latest troop deployment. And more than 60% said they feared that the Gulf would 'bog down
and become another Vietnam.'"

Part I

1

Alexis de Tocqueville

Alexis de Tocqueville, philosopher and politician, was intensely a man of his class: a hereditary member of the territorial aristocracy upon whose fidelity the French monarchy had rested for ten centuries; the aristocracy that had survived, diminished yet unbowed, the French Revolution, the Jacobin terror, and the Napoleonic dictatorship. He was not a democrat by education or personal association. He owed his seat in the Chamber of the July monarchy to the vote of the country squires of his district, a corner of traditionally conservative Normandy. That franchise, severely hedged in by property qualifications, left the bulk of the urban working class unrepresented.

It is thus a measure of Tocqueville's lucid detachment from ancestral sentiment and self-interest that he, loyal monarchist and irreconcilable foe of populism in all its guises, foresaw, long before the great builders of systems, the fall of privilege, the rise of the masses, the triumph of democracy in the West, and its clash with despotism from the East. A man of the Old Regime, Tocqueville assessed what he had observed in America, looked ahead, and concluded that there would be no place in the order he saw emerging for the class to which he belonged. But he did not write as a partisan; he wrote as a prophet, like all great historians.

His American Visit

Alexis de Tocqueville's American visit lasted less than one year. During his travels, he managed to accumulate meticulously a mass of information not only about American prisons and prison reform—this being the official mission assigned to him by the French government that granted him leave from his magisterial duties—but also about the state

7

of American society fifty years after its accession to sovereign state-hood, a republic and a democracy by the free choice of its citizens. That the Republic had survived so long; that the monarchies and principalities, then ruling all of Europe and its empires overseas, had failed to bring it down; and that liberated America prospered, this perplexed the most astute minds of the times. But by the time he left America, it no longer perplexed Alexis de Tocqueville.

Yet, this was merely the beginning of Tocqueville's great achievement. What Tocqueville drew from his understanding of the American phenomenon was an understanding of America as the first step in a great transformation of Western society: the rout of autocracy, on one hand, and, on the other hand, the advance of popular sovereignty—not everywhere honoring the rules of democracy in action, but almost everywhere in speech. Having rigorously analyzed the forces of change, Tocqueville predicted that their sweep would be universal. What had happened in America, he concluded, was not a development unique to a settlement of European emigrés at the margins of European empire, but a bold step into a future that beckoned all of mankind.

In this way, Tocqueville became the first European thinker who—his celebrated case study in hand—presented a model of the dynamics of a live democracy and defined the issues that would confront all democracies, living and dead: the ceaseless struggles between nationalism and liberalism; between egalitarianism and individualism; and, on a global scale, between autocracy and democracy.

Tocqueville and France

When Tocqueville returned to France, he could see the course of European politics following as an evident conclusion from these premises. Thus, it was simple for Tocqueville to predict that the July monarchy—that caricature of a monarchy drawn so mercilessly by Honoré Daumier[1]—would not last; that the raffish greed and self-destructive lack of foresight of the bourgeoisie-in-power would trigger countervailing forces; and that those countervailing forces would in turn bring down the established order, not only in Tocqueville's native France but in all of Europe.

Of course, Tocqueville did not foresee the specific chain reaction of revolution and reaction, the great civil wars of the twentieth century. No one could have. But Tocqueville was certain of the outcome: the future belonged to democracy. The idea that he had seen regnant in America would sweep the world.

As a political philosopher, Tocqueville elucidated the changes that he deemed inevitable. As a man of the world, he espoused them. The leaders of English liberalism were Tocqueville's friends;[2] his principles, in the round, were theirs—which placed him on the side of parliamentary democracy. He was close enough to the generation that had suffered the nationalist ravages of mob rule and despotism, under the French Revolution and the Bonapartist dictatorship, to dread the propensity of history to repeat itself.

Perhaps this explains the sense of urgency that drives Tocqueville's exploration of democracy *in situ* and the publication of his findings. In the 1830s, France was as deeply divided as it had been in the 1780s, mired in complacency and pettiness, incapable of meeting the challenges of the age, and lacking in political reforms (such as Lord Grey's parliamentary reforms in England).[3] Tocqueville worried about what such drift portended, and we now know Tocqueville was right to worry. Political lethargy left French society defenseless, in 1850, against a power grab by a bold adventurer who staked his gamble on the appeal of the grandeur lost—and of the great name.[4]

Forthrightly, and at some risk, Tocqueville continued to profess an uncompromising adherence to his liberal principles.[5] In the pages of a journal he had founded, he took his stand vocally on the side of electoral reform and denounced the crass cupidity of the ruling classes. He inveighed against the populist dictatorship of Louis-Napoleon, and suffered for it. Indeed, Louis-Napoleon started his career as plebiscitary dictator by jailing Tocqueville, together with other members of the Chamber. Then he was deprived of all political office for refusing his oath to the new regime. Tocqueville's credentials as a man of the Republican Left are impeccable.

When Tocqueville sought to re-enter politics, he did so by publishing another book, *L'Ancien Régime et la Révolution Francaise,* which continued his theme of liberty and democracy. Tocqueville's life's work should thus be seen as a continuum, with *Democracy in America* as merely the first step in an unrelenting search that ended, literally, at his deathbed in 1859.

But posterity, though it fulsomely acknowledges the brilliance of Tocqueville's early case study, has not been kind to the evolution of his thought. Perhaps it is a measure of our infatuation with predictions, more or less scientific, that Tocqueville owes much of his latter-day fame to prophecies, and to the book where those prophecies were made.

Nevertheless, *Democracy in America* is *not* the masterpiece that contains the essence of Tocqueville's philosophy, and he himself did not think so. For more than twenty years after *Democracy* appeared in print, Tocqueville kept probing the enigma of power in a society of free men. *L'Ancien Régime et la Révolution Francaise* was the result, and it was the magnum opus of his maturity, a powerful, yet measured indictment of French society before the Revolution, as well as the failure of the men who made the revolution to tame and direct the forces they themselves had set free. Its relevancy to the great transformation that swept across Western society in the wake of two World Wars, is both baneful and striking.

But though he was a great prophet of democracy, Tocqueville was too astute an observer to harbor any illusions about the place of his own class in a liberal state. The Great Revolution had broken the back of the old order, the French nation of the ancien régime. The enfranchisement of the masses, he concluded—a touch balefully—would sweep away what was left of it. Like another great noble a hundred years later, he had concluded that democracy was not a perfect form of government, but the least imperfect; of all forms of government, the least flawed.

Notes

1. Honoré(-Victorin) Daumier, 1808-79, was a prolific French caricaturist, painter, and sculptor. In 1832, he was sentenced to six months in prison for attacking the Orleanist monarchy in his cartoons. Later, he refused to accept decoration from the Empire of Louis Napoleon.
2. Among them were the philosopher and economist John Stuart Mill (1806-1873), and Nassau William Senior (1790-1864), the British classical economist and author of *An Outline of the Science of Political Economy.*
3. Charles Grey, 2d Earl Grey, was British prime minister from 1830 to 1834 and oversaw the Reform Act of 1832, which dealt with the House of Commons. The act abolished old and created new parliamentary boroughs in an attempt to establish something like a rough representation according to population. In effect, the Reform Act of 1832 "ensured that the new State should...be partially democratized at the centre." See David Thomson, *England in the 19th Century* (Baltimore, Md.: Penguin Books, 1950), p. 73.
4. "Louis' sole source of strength was the immense popularity of his name among the mass of the people with whom as yet he had come into no personal contact at

all." J.P.T. Bury, *France 1814–1940* (London: Methuen and Co., Ltd., 1969), p. 15.

5. In a letter to the editor of *The Times,* published December 11, 1851, Tocqueville indicted the new regime, writing: "Human life is as little respected as human liberty." He called Louis-Napoleon's appeal to the people an "odious mockery," and noted the paradox of simultaneously calling on public opinion and establishing a "military terrorism throughout the country." See J.P. Mayer, *Alexis de Tocqueville, A Biographical Study* (Gloucester, Mass.: Harper and Brothers, 1966), p. 62.

2

Tocqueville and Nationalism

Tocqueville, a tireless correspondent, wrote thousands of letters, and some of his deepest thoughts lie hidden in these missives to friends, themselves masters of that literary genre that is as typically French as the conversation of clever men and beautiful women. Among Tocqueville's letters are those to his friend Count Joseph Arthur Gobineau[1]—who was first a French diplomat in Teheran and then Tocqueville's chief-of-cabinet during the latter's brief tenure as foreign minister of France. The contents of these letters touch upon some of the most profound issues of liberalism, nationalism, and race.

For the Liberal nationalists who, in Europe, manned the barricades of the 1830s and 1840s, "the nation" and "liberalism" were two sides of the same coin: nationhood was the due of a cultural community democratically governed and mindful of the common interests of mankind.

Today, we know, nationalism and liberalism are no longer companions but enemies. In our times, nationalism, the gross caricature of a noble idea, is restrained neither by liberal constitutions nor by concern for the common interests of mankind. It is checked only by superior power; it has become the school for violence and dictatorship. It is narrowly parochial; it impedes the exchanges of goods and ideas and thus stunts economic and cultural growth. Nationalism has turned into the greatest retrogressive force of this century. It is now the deadly enemy of liberalism.

Tocqueville's sharp eye discerned the mortal danger to liberalism from the distortion of the ideals that were leading nationalism to victory: the degradation of love of country into hatred of diversity, of patriotism into chauvinism, of equality of conditions into the inequalities enforced by the military state.

In his letters to Tocqueville, Gobineau argued that the moral warrant of nationalism is the superiority of one people over all others, be it by virtue of the purity of its race and, failing the test of consanguinity, the purity of its culture, made manifest in its common language. In this way, his correspondence with Tocqueville anticipates the opening of the abyss that, fifty years later, was to cleave French society and, in the twentieth century, was to bring on the murderous totalitarian wars of class and race.

Tocqueville, a polite man, responded politely to Gobineau, but began by politely taking apart Gobineau's scholarly pretensions. He went on to warn Gobineau of the destructive force latent in the racist ideology. Racism and populism are kin, he declared. Whatever they might be in theory, and no matter how much they might differ in their respective rhetoric, they have always been as one in their hostility to the open society. Historically, too, the extremes of racism and populism have tended to fuse in that critical mass called the Nation, which, when provoked even by seemingly minor events, can shatter civility.

Nationalism in the Twentieth Century

Nationalism, as I have noted above, is a simple idea. That is its strength. Military power, in its application, is also simple and crude. That is why nationalism finds its natural ally in militarism. When responsible government has failed to gratify popular expectations and, minimally, to defend the realm and to maintain order in the streets, then men will seek salvation in the companionship of all and everybody—the nation. Nationalism is thus the ideology of failure.

Stalin's government, though masked by an ineffably complex ideology invented by bellicose civilians, was in essence a nationalist military dictatorship, primitive and crude. The governments that preceded and followed his were also nationalist military dictatorships, albeit to differing extents. That is why a people, for seventy years habituated to military discipline, now is baffled, if not repelled, by the voluntarism that is the lifeblood of democracy.

How the Soviet peoples responded to Stalin's nationalist appeals (and to similar appeals earlier and later) is a story that has, to this day, not been fully told. We do know that, in the hour of supreme crisis, Stalin reached into Russia's past for symbols of martial valor. The Orders of

Suvorov and Kutusov, named after the victors over the Napoleonic armies, rewarded the heroism of Soviet warriors. When Hitler's forces stood at the gates of Moscow, Stalin unabashedly called not on the proletariat but on the Russian people, and he called on them to defend the Motherland rather than the vanguard of the working class and the verities of Marxist-Leninist doctrine. In response, the Russian people rose to arms. They wore—and wore proudly—the emblems of their military service; they died by the millions in the defense of Mother Russia. Even the Red Army's ethnic minorities—Russia's vassals—did not shirk their duties to the Russo-Soviet state, though not all of them responded as fervently to the appeals of this synthetic Soviet nationalism as did their comrades of Russian stock.[2]

The Soviet case is not unique. Can it be seriously argued that millions of Chinese fought and died in the Ten Years' War against Japan for the cause of Marxism? China's intelligentsia barely managed to decipher the writings of Marx, Engels, and Lenin. Without Mao's surgery, *Das Kapital* would have been totally incomprehensible to the great mass of the Chinese people. In both the Soviet Union and Maoist China, it was grassroots nationalism and not Marxist ideology that won the day.

Today, wherever a similar militaristic nationalism appears, it, too, may espouse a similar mishmash of collectivist doctrines, leftover from discredited communism, for the intellectual respectability that it so conspicuously lacks in the marketplaces of ideas. Thus, for example, the Syrian and the Iraqi ruling elites profess themselves to be inspired by the secular philosophy of Ba'thism, tailored to Marxist specifications, hence secular and collectivist. Certainly, the devotion of these Syrian and Iraqi elites to Islam is marginal—although that does not mean they will not make the most of their observance of Muslim rites for public relations purposes. In fact, however, both the Syrian and Iraqi governments are intensely nationalist—even to the point of detesting one another, fellow Ba'athists though they may be. Likewise, the Arab nation generally, never more than a dream, is now a dream that has been dispelled, from Tangier to the Straits of Oman.[3]

As for the call of fundamentalism: nowhere have the Muslim masses heeded the call to Jihad. Iran stands alone as a Muslim theocratic state, and the Iranians, not being Arabs, are disqualified from putting the supranational community of Islam together again.

Amid this spiritual vacuum, nationalism is reemerging, here and now, and all over the world. It is ubiquitous, and no people, including the charter members of the New World Order themselves, including the United States, are immune from it. Though widely believed to have faded away in the last fifty years, or to have taken on merely quaint and acceptable forms, nationalism has in fact been muting its true nature while the industrialized world struggled to find more sophisticated, rational ways of ordering its affairs. Today, nationalism is reasserting itself and gaining ground with ever increasing speed, reawakening atavistic and disruptive passions wherever it appears.

The Remedy

Tocqueville thought this catastrophe need not happen, for he did not underrate the latent strengths of a liberal society. Indeed, he believed that in America the outcome of the democratic experiment was settled. There, the foundations of liberalism had been soundly laid, and Americans would keep on strengthening the democratic institutions that they had so recently put in the place of monarchical privilege.

In Europe, however, a thousand years of feudalism would render the emergence of liberalism more tortuous—and more doubtful. Tocqueville's *Ancien Régime et la Révolution Française* tells us how close the French nation had come to being torn apart by revolution and counterrevolution, and how ambiguous had been the bequest of the Great Revolution that cast up the Napoleonic Empire.

Sensitive to the tensions wracking French society, he warned his countrymen against the threats posed by, on the one side, Rousseau's mob-nation, and, on the other, an aristocratic state of privilege, hallowed by tradition and religious belief. Personally, Tocqueville never wavered in his belief that liberalism could triumph over both.

But if the contagion is to be stopped, prophylactic measures will have to be taken at once—they should have been taken years ago. And this means that the American people will have to join in a foreign policy aimed at stopping nationalism. In a democratic state, foreign policy begins at home. To make such a foreign policy, however, the American people will first have to be asked to silence their immediate needs with a view of the future, something that does not come naturally to a democratic people.[4]

Notes

1. Joseph-Arthur, comte de Gobineau (1816–82), "French diplomat, writer, ethnologist, and social thinker whose theory of racial determinism had an enormous influence upon the subsequent development of racist theories and practices in western Europe.... [I]t was his *Essai sur l'inégalité des races humaines,* 4 vol. (1853–55; *Essay on the Inequality of the Human Races,* new ed. 1967) that was by far his most influential work." *The New Encyclopaedia Britannica,* s.v. "Gobineau."
2. In 1991, Dale R. Herspring, a professor of Russian area studies at Georgetown University, after detailing the ethnic problems in the Soviet military, cited one Soviet officer's opinion that they were the most serious problems confronting the Soviet military. See Dale R. Herspring, "The Soviet Military Reshapes in Response to Malaise," *Orbis,* Spring 1991, p. 182, citing "Internatsional'nomy vospitaniy—bol'she partiynogo vnimaniya," *Kommunist vooruzhennykh sil,* March 1989, p. 9.
3. See Mahmud Faksh, "Withered Arab Nationalism," *Orbis,* Summer 1993, pp. 425–38.
4. Alexis de Tocqueville, "How, When Conditions Are Equal and Skepticism Is Rife, It Is Important to Direct Human Actions to Distant Objects," in *Democracy in America,* vol. 2, ed. Phillips Bradley (New York: Vintage Books, 1945), pp. 158–60.

3

Tocqueville and Hedonism

Throughout history, two concepts of civic life have vied with one another: austerity and hedonism. Among societies dedicated to the ideal of austerity, ancient Sparta, Republican Rome, Puritan Massachusetts, and Frederican Prussia are, perhaps, the most celebrated examples. Among societies dedicated to hedonism, late Imperial Rome has gone down in history as the most notorious case of self-destruction through overindulgence.

Only rarely does an individual man attain the absolute of these alternative concepts of life: only the saint rises above all temptations of the flesh; only the degenerate succumbs to all of them. No social norm has ever reached an absolute, and no social fabric has ever been a seamless web: no doubt, some Spartans hankered after un-Spartan comforts, and not all citizens of late Rome were content to loll about for the rest of their lives in the public bath, feasting on free meals supplied by imperial munificence.

Most societies throughout history have swung between the two extremes. Some, however, have shaped their mores closely enough to the austere model of Sparta, and others have clutched frivolously enough at the joys of Sybaritic self-indulgence, to allow for some generalizations: an austere society is apt to be more long-lived than a hedonistic one, and the former is likely to win out in a contest with the latter, even allowing for a considerable inferiority of the former's material resources.

More important still, a hedonist society is more likely to surrender its liberties to rulers who dole out the necessities of life and the luxuries of leisure, and who ask nothing in return but to be left to rule. An austere society that husbands its resources for the sake of future achievements, though it might forgive its rulers not a few vices, will not stand for institutionalized profligacy. Even more important and more simple still, the Hedonist ethos legitimizes consumption as the highest civic virtue; the ethos of austerity acclaims service to the community—the industry and the valor of the citizenry, self-discipline, and self-denial of the individual—as the highest social goods.

Hedonistic societies seem to be relatively short-lived, which is not to say that they are culturally barren: beautiful plants grow from decaying matter. But politically they have proved highly perishable.

The logic is simple. A hedonistic society tends ineluctably to a state of anomie, the alienation of the individual from society. This is a fact noted by historians from Tacitus to Toynbee. The condition of anomie, in turn, leads to the surrender of individual civic responsibility, and so to despotism, either in the form of an irremovable ruling class or of an absolute ruler, mostly the latter.

Since a hedonistic society is, by definition, a society governed by unlimited individual demands for material enjoyment, the ruling class derives its legitimacy from an ability to satisfy unlimited individual demands at no cost in collective exertions. And since this is logically impossible, the ruling class is forced to contrive the appearance of doing the impossible—by robbing Peter to pay Paul.

It is at this point that the ethics of egalitarianism enters to justify the political economics of hedonism. Since it is logically impossible to equalize the innate endowments of all men to a common norm, and so to equalize their proper reward, the egalitarian state is forced to equalize rewards for unequal achievements—an endless process of cutting Peter down to the size of Paul.

Hedonism and America

In the early days of the Republic, American society tended to give its allegiance to the ideal of the austere society. Some, perhaps most, of the Founders had been reared in the history of Republican Rome. Thomas Jefferson explicitly hailed a commonwealth similar to Fabius Cunctator's Rome as the ideal state—a commonwealth of independent farmers, none too rich and none too poor. "Those who labor in the earth," Jefferson wrote, "are the chosen people of God, if ever He had a chosen people, whose breasts He has made His peculiar deposit for substantial and genuine virtue."[1]

The young Republic did not quite measure up to Jefferson's utopia. Yet it came close enough to impress Alexis de Tocqueville. The astute Frenchman noted the American's propensity for hard work and vigorous exertion, his strong sense of community, and his firm attachment to his rights under law. From these observations, Tocqueville filtered his concept of freedom and equality—or rather of what Americans then meant by these concepts. What they meant was inseparable from what they understood to be their national ethos. We might disagree on the consistency of that national ethos and the average man's understanding of it, but, for a certainty, the dominant ethos of American society was not hedonistic.

The same categoric assurance cannot be given for contemporary American society. The slogans of the commercial advertisers and of the political champions of the redistributive mission of the state extol an ideal of the good life that Tocqueville's Americans would have deemed sharply at odds with their understanding of the good life. However difficult it is to enter the psyches of men and women who lived two hundred years ago, their recorded utterances—in literature, political debate, and statements of religious faith—leave no doubt that they did not consider the average citizen's capacity for consuming material goods and enjoying leisure as the mark of civic worth. In contemporary America, by contrast, individual appetites are silencing appeals to that continence that, for the sake of man's spiritual and bodily health, must govern his sensuality. America has travelled far enough down the road of social anomie to discern the unmistakable syndrome of hedonism and egalitarianism.

The Transformation

Alexis de Tocqueville anticipated this change in the American ethos. But how? Principally through his skepticism concerning democracy's capacity for self-denial, for he noted uneasily democracy's propensity for gratifying the "immediate needs" of the great mass of people, rather than bearing with austerity in order to enjoy the blessings of greater security and prosperity later.

> The first thing that strikes the observation [in America] is an innumerable multitude of men, all equal and alike, incessantly endeavoring to procure the petty and paltry pleasures with which they glut their lives.[2]

For better or worse, Tocqueville's analytical tools did not include macroeconomic theory, and so he has nothing of consequence to say about the Republic's budgetary policies. Yet, in this field, too, Tocqueville's reflections on the likely evolution of American democracy are uncanny in their presentiment of the future. Starting from the observation quoted above, and reasoning as a political philosopher, Tocqueville anticipates the rise of the welfare state—the state that the mass of the people expect to take care of their lifetime needs, not to speak of their immediate ones.

> Above this race of men stands an immense and tutelary power, which takes upon itself alone to secure their gratifications and to watch over their fate. That power is absolute, minute, regular, provident, and mild. It would be like the authority of a parent, if, like that authority, its object was to prepare men for manhood; but it seeks, on the contrary, to keep them in perpetual childhood: it is well content that the people should rejoice, provided that they think of nothing but rejoicing.[3]

Tocqueville's description of the welfare state's rise is incisive, but he is not arguing against democracy on those grounds. Tocqueville observes; he records; he projects. In a time of virulent ideological controversies in Europe, his commentary on the strengths and weaknesses of democracy remains, throughout the full length of his book, scrupulously impartial and undogmatic.

So far, however, one must concede that Tocqueville has been right. Bureaucratization of life and a proliferation of public drones are sapping the spontaneity and self-reliance that, so it seemed to Tocqueville, constitute the strongest traits of the American character. A dismal record of inflation, fiscal incontinence, and lack of discipline have cast a long shadow over democracy. Indeed, none of the great democracies can be said to have bitten the bullet of austerity in order to settle accounts, rather than leave this unpleasant task to another generation. The only halt in this historic retreat from fiscal probity has been in times of war, for the exigencies of war wonderfully clear a people's mind and "silence its immediate needs with a view of the future."[4]

Is there a way back? History does not offer cheering analogies. It suggests that either there will be no turning back, or that the passage back will be a rough one, beginning only when challenges currently unforeseen compel our peoples to recall the virtues that, in Tocqueville's lifetime, made them great. Nevertheless, Americans are a savvy people;

eventually, we may hope, they will become mistrustful of politicians bearing redistributive gifts.

Notes

1. Thomas Jefferson, *Notes on the State of Virginia (1781–85)* (Boston, Mass.: H. Sprague, 1802), p. 226.
2. Alexis de Tocqueville, *Democracy in America,* vol. 2, ed. Phillips Bradley (New York: Vintage Books, 1945), p. 336.
3. Ibid.
4. Tocqueville, "How, When Conditions Are Equal and Skepticism Is Rife, It Is Important to Direct Human Actions to Distant Objects," in *Democracy in America,* vol. 2, pp. 158-60.

4

Tocqueville and World Conflict

If there was one issue that nineteenth-century European liberals—who passionately divided on many issues—could passionately agree upon, it was their deep mistrust of the emperor of Russia. They had good reason. Alexander I prided himself on being the architect and leader of the Holy Alliance.[1] He bequeathed this diplomatic edifice to his heir, Nikolaus I, a man more orderly, though more narrow in thought and more brutal in application than his fey predecessor.

The Holy Alliance, demystified, served as the instrument of monarchical reaction against the forces set free by the French Revolution and its aftermath, the Napoleonic Wars. Although much about the French Revolution, we can now see, was ambiguous or downright counterproductive, it did mark the first and giant step towards representative government and, hence, democracy in Europe.

Napoleon sought to snuff out the flame ignited by the French Revolution. But his legions bore the torch to the lands they conquered. They set Europe afire. Napoleon, himself, was the victim of the ensuing conflagration. So were some of his fellow monarchs—monarchs of antecedents more venerable than his.

Thus, the watchword of the Holy Alliance was "legitimacy," the defense of the dynastic order wherever it had survived the firestorm of the Revolution, and its restoration wherever it had been brought low. The strongest and least scathed of the survivors was czarist Russia, the epitome of monarchical absolutism. Moreover, the czars brought to the alliance of princes what it needed most in its effort to make reaction stick: the largest standing army in Europe.

Russian Imperialism

No wonder Tocqueville's Europe stood in fear of Russia. When Napoleon fell, Russia occupied and plundered a good part of the continent, including some of the principalities allied with it in the cause of legitimacy. Many years and heavy diplomatic labor were required to ease the czar's soldiers out of the "zones of occupation," or, rather, some of them. And even those troops withdrawn were not disbanded.

Thus, Tocqueville and most Frenchmen viewed the armies of Russia as a grave and present danger to Europe's security. Allowing for the logistics of the times, they stood in easy marching distance from most of the capitals of Europe. They were eager to march, perhaps more eager than the czars, blood relatives of most European rulers, and, like Alexander I himself, capable of toying with the ideas of European liberalism.

The Russian military, except for a few high aristocrats educated by expensive European schoolmasters, were unquestioning in their fidelity to the principles of autocratic rule, though not always to the person of the ruler. They stood ready to defend Holy Mother Russia against the Jacobins and their godless armies. They wanted to fight, this being their calling; and, if there was nothing to fight for in Europe, they meant to fight in the East. Thus, in Tocqueville's time, the pace of Russian imperialism quickened.

After the Napoleonic Wars, Russia increased her pressure on the Ottoman Empire, prematurely alleged to be moribund and due for dismemberment. England, France, and Austria demurred at this solution of the Eastern Problem. Tortuous as were their policies, and bitter as were their rivalries, they came to agree on one issue: the Bosporus had to be blocked against a Russian foray into the warm waters.

In Tocqueville's lifetime, this conflict of incompatible strategic interests culminated in the Crimean War, which czarist Russia lost. Compensating for its defeat, Russia increased its military pressures on the Caucasus and Central Asia, and accelerated the colonization of its dominions in the East and Far East of Asia, setting the stage for a century of cold war between Russia and England, and a hot war between Russia and Japan.

Russia and America

In 1821, when Tocqueville was but fifteen years of age, Russia attempted by ukase, the rescript-without-appeal of the autocrat, to exclude foreign navigators from the Bering Sea and the Pacific Coast of its possessions. In response, the United States and Great Britain immediately protested.

The outcome was a treaty with the United States in 1824, and with Great Britain in 1825, by which Russia relinquished some of its more extravagant claims. These treaties established the boundaries of Russia's Pacific possessions. From then on out, much was to happen, ravelling and unravelling the skein of the contenders' diplomatic relationships. But the gist of this long and complicated story is simple, and could not have escaped a mind as sharp as Tocqueville's: the czarist empire (a despotic state with a huge army and a redemptory mission) and the American Republic (a democracy bent on trade rather than military conquest) had met in the fogs of the northern waters.

What was his response? No doubt, it would be gratifying to Tocqueville's latter-day admirers if it could be shown that he deplored the evils of colonialism that marred the advance of Western civilization and did not leave unscathed the American Republic. But that is not the case. It took the West another hundred years to apprehend these evils, not to speak of eradicating them root and branch. Tocqueville heartily approved of France's colonial ventures in Arab North Africa, and he viewed the westward expansion of the United States as a natural, healthy development, the consequence of the rapid growth of the Republic's population. Free men, seeking room for settlement in the vast spaces of the Continent, pushed forward the frontiers of the Republic and, in the event, the sway of its institutions.

But what Tocqueville did grasp was the difference between the kind of rule that czarist absolutism and American democracy, respectively, were likely to impose on their imperial acquisitions. And it was this difference between Russia and America, an ideological difference, not strategic proximity, that Tocqueville thought was likely to lead to a collision between the two powers.

Of all the Great Powers, he found Russia least likely to embrace democracy, its people least capable to strike out by themselves on the road to political freedom. Hence, so he concluded, the tension between the world's most powerful despotism and the world's most spacious democracy could not but increase, foreshadowing a global collision.

Of course, Tocqueville's well-informed guess was borne out, though little in the world scene of his day appeared to lend it credence. If his American interlocutors were worried about the presence of Russian imperialism in the Pacific region, they did not tell him so. On issues of global politics, American public opinion at this time tended to side with Russia, the principal counterweight to Britain in world politics. Indeed, much later, in 1867, the geographical differences of the American and Russian governments were reconciled, when the czar sold his colony, Alaska, to the United States at a derisory price.[2]

But Tocqueville, keen as was his understanding of geographical realities, viewed the confrontation of two political systems—democracy and despotism—as the likely cause of war between Russia and the American Republic. The word "ideology" (a coinage of eighteenth-century France) is absent from the text of *Democracy in America,* but its author evidently was not indifferent to the power of ideas as the prime movers of history. Sooner or later, he saw, America's "plough share" would run up against Russia's "sword." Thither the relationship of the two irreconcilable protagonists was trending—even if they themselves did not know it.

The Future of the Conflict

A wide consensus exists in the councils of Western governments, the Western press, and Western academic circles that the breakdown of the Soviet empire is irreversible. But is it? Do the autonomies, granted or tolerated by Moscow, spell the Russian Republic's renunciation of imperialism?

I will return to the discussion of this question below. Here it may suffice to invoke the history of Russia, a vast and multi-ethnic country locked in ceaseless battle against centrifugal forces. Despite many setbacks—some of them as bloody as the bloodiest massacres perpetrated by Russia's imperial rulers, from the Czars Ivan and Peter to Nicholas II —the Russian genius for endurance and limitless sacrifice has kept the Soviet empire together for seventy years.

Both the czarist and the Soviet rulers of the empire were uncompromisingly Russian nationalists. Are their Russian successors, who vow themselves democrats, less conscious of the greatness and the power of the Russian nation? It is not likely that 150 million intelligent, vigorous, and disciplined people will resign themselves to being the supplicants of Western largesse. Certainly, whoever rules Russia will tap the immense latent force of patriotism that has raised Russia from defeat and humiliation in 1812, 1904–5, 1917, and 1942.

Suppose, however, that democratic Russia is prepared to retreat from the imperial goals of predecessors. Suppose, this time, the Kremlin retreats peacefully from the pre-perestroika limits of its power, and evinces no intention to assert itself again as a world power. Does that brighten the prospects of East-West relations? Not necessarily. If any of history's teachings is unarguable, it is that empires are most dangerous when they begin to crumble. The experience of czarist Russia bears that out.

Notes

1. The Holy Alliance was a loose organization of European sovereigns, formed by Alexander I of Russia, Francis I of Austria, and Frederick William III of Prussia on September 26, 1815, in order to promote Christian principles in the affairs of nations.
2. Alaska was sold to the United States in 1867 for $7,200,000. Since the total federal budget that year, apart from debt repayment, was $357,500,000, the cost to the U.S. government was on the order of 2 percent of the budget (apart from debt repayment). Using that same measure, a comparable figure in the early 1990s might be $25 billion. The czar's willingness to sell Alaska was apparently motivated by two factors: Russia's military defeat in the Crimean War (1853–56) and the near-extinction of the sea otter, whose fur had previously been the chief economic value produced by Alaska.

5

Tocqueville and Equality

The development of democracy in the United States will determine not only the kind of state that governs America but also the political order—democratic or undemocratic—that governs the world. The period of grace for this determination is likely to be as long as the time it took to bring down communist despotism: two or three generations. But victory presupposes that American democracy remains as vigorous as Tocqueville found it.

Alexis de Tocqueville came to America to study the new, democratic Republic. He departed confident of its universal drawing power, but not without reservations of its future health.

On the first point, history has confirmed Tocqueville's judgment. Notwithstanding America's evolution from a small nation of farmers and merchants of farm produce to an urban-industrial giant, the Republic remains—to a degree surpassing Tocqueville's boldest expectations— the admitted or unadmitted ideal of the world. Intermittent bouts of malaise have not dimmed its luster, and the reason is easily found. Compared to much of the world's population, if not to their own forefathers, Americans are relatively free: they still govern themselves; they are equal before the law; temperamentally, they are jealous of their rights; and, despite an ever more invasive government, they exercise many rights.

As for the future health of the American system: Tocqueville's reservations reflected his doubts about America's ability to keep united the two forces that created it: man's aspirations for freedom and his aspiration for equality. *Democracy in America* celebrates, even as it questions, the fine balance of these primordial forces, as Tocqueville found that balance during his American travels. Because nothing has happened in the confines of American democracy that might assure the country's

31

ability (or inability) to sustain this equipoise between liberty and democracy, Tocqueville's book remains timely. The issue is still in doubt. The American people are still free to debate it, and, for better or worse, to resolve it to determine their fate—and thus the world's.

Democracy and Equality

The writings of Alexis de Tocqueville reflect an uncanny sensitivity to the forces that threaten democracy in America, forces that threaten all democracies, and that will threaten democracy wherever it strikes roots. Of course, Tocqueville was not unmindful that other dangers to American democracy exist. He knew that democracy is not exempt from the infections that sicken all government: the rulers' hypocrisy and lust for power; the masses' brutality and fecklessness. But Tocqueville—a visitor from Europe's society of castes and classes—was more impressed by dangers specific to a democratic state, notably egalitarianism, than by such traditional dangers as a nostalgia for the pomp and panoply of monarchical rule.

Thus, in his introduction to *Democracy in America,* Tocqueville wrote:

> Amongst the novel objects that attracted my attention during my stay in the United States, nothing struck me more forcibly than the general equality of condition among the people. I readily discovered the prodigious influence which this primary fact exercises on the whole course of society; it gives a peculiar direction to public opinion, and a peculiar tenor to the laws; it imparts new maxims to the governing authorities, and peculiar habits to the governed.

> I soon perceived that the influence of this fact extends far beyond the political character and the laws of the country, and that it has no less empire over civil society than over the government; it creates opinions, gives birth to new sentiments, founds novel customs, and modifies whatever it does not produce. The more I advanced in the study of American society, the more I perceived that this equality of condition is the fundamental fact from which all others seem to be derived, and the central point at which all my observations constantly terminated.[1]

In his aversion to egalitarianism, Tocqueville was not alone.[2] He was, however, one of the first observers of America's democracy-at-work to perceive the tension between liberty and democracy latent in the country's perfection of the democratic process: politically, American democracy could offer no remedy to the absolute rule of the majority, no safeguard against the absolute subjection of the minority. Thus, the end of liberty could happen quite peaceably and in a quite orderly fashion. At the end of the day, the minority could be voted out of existence, and the conformity of all to all could be voted in. Indeed, at the end of the day, the rule of the majority could be voted out of existence, in perfect conformity with democratic procedure. Democracy is the only form of government that can commit suicide.[3]

This was a central problem for democracy that Tocqueville felt he had to confront, not only for abstract reasons but for very practical ones as well. As I noted in the first chapter, *Democracy in America* is a didactic work. It was meant to show, by holding up the American example, a way out of the disarray of French politics. Of course, Tocqueville knew the American model would not fit France. But he believed Frenchmen could learn from it—from America's great achievements as well as its defects.

By 1830, the latter were becoming more apparent as the American Republic, growing in self-confidence, launched itself on the conquest of an empire. The nation's conduct was increasingly at odds with the high moral principles enshrined in the great documents composed at Philadelphia. Andrew Jackson's America was not a school of manners. The citizens that came to Washington to see their chosen representatives at work did not observe the niceties of polite society.

Yet, the exuberance of populism was also a sign of health—the spontaneity of a simple and egalitarian society. There were differences of wealth in the United States, but they were not as great or as ostentatious as in the old countries of Europe. Undivided by class, Americans of the Jacksonian era lived with one another in a boisterous bonhomie, thereby achieving a civic concord that still eluded France.

Tocqueville was never able to deduce from his case study the right balance between the idea of liberty and the idea of equality, but he knew civilization required one. Much less was he able to say how a proper balance could be maintained if it were achieved in the first place. Historically, Tocqueville saw that the principle of equality—equality of condition—had been and continued to be the *idée force*—the demiurge—of modern history. "In running over the pages of our history for seven hundred years," he writes, "we shall scarcely find a single great event which has not promoted equality of condition."[4]

Perhaps if Tocqueville failed to find the appropriate balance between liberty and equality, it is because such a balance is unattainable, and democracy is fated to swing forever between the absolute of freedom—anarchy—and the absolute of equality—conformity.

At any rate, Tocqueville did see that the problem cannot be solved by institutional devices, within the confines of a democracy, and that the American democracy therefore depended for its health on the people's deference to moral precepts and civic virtues beyond the range of politics. These, in turn, depended for their observation upon the activities of freely flourishing, private associations, such as the religious, charitable, and cultural, that kindled the communal spirit, set standards of civic behavior—and kept politics at bay. Today, these associations still remain the guardians of American freedom against the danger that matters most.[5]

At the end of the twentieth century, the United States is unlikely, even when subjected to domestic crisis and foreign peril, to surrender itself to a despotic executive. For that, we may rely upon the people's respect for their Constitution. We may rely, too, upon those legions of lawyers and judges who stand ready to use the Constitution—sometimes too quickly—against an assertive government. Not least, we may rely upon the Congress, which stands ready—often all too quickly—to restrain the power of the executive, impressions of the media to the contrary notwithstanding.

In short, the danger of Bonapartism, the danger that an American fuehrer will come to power in Washington, the danger that "it" will, after all, "happen here" is chimerical.[6] Rather, the most insidious threat to freedom in America today is from a paternalist state bent upon enforcing conformity, conformity being, by definition, intolerant. As for the pretense of diversity where none exists, so common today, this is but the characteristic propaganda of conformity.

Over a hundred and fifty years ago, Tocqueville discerned that such conformity would be the gravest of dangers to our democracy, because conformity derives from the very feature that sets democracy apart from all other systems of government: the unchecked rule of the majority. "Democratic institutions," Tocqueville wrote, "awaken and foster a passion for equality which they can never satisfy."[7]

But in the America of the 1830s, the issue was not yet worrisome. A happy mix of political institutions, private interests, and civic morality kept the passions of the populace in bounds. The majoritarian threat to freedom still seemed a bogey that need not distract American democracy from its dedicaton to equality before the law.

It could never be that for Tocqueville, whose family had suffered the atrocities of the French Revolution. Although he himself was born after the Terror, images of Jacobin massacres and mob rule—both claiming plausibly to derive their authority from the majoritarian will of the people—had been impressed on his mind for life.

And so Tocqueville worried about America's individualist soul. Presciently, we now know. A hundred and fifty years later, the egalitarian thrust has lost nothing of its vigor in America. The trend towards social equality seems irresistible. The most powerful motive force in American politics is redistribution of wealth. And the most powerful idea in American political philosophy is the Procustean bed of egalitarianism and redistribution.

Notes

1. Alexis de Tocqueville, *Democracy in America,* vol. 1, ed. Phillips Bradley (New York: Vintage Books, 1945), p. 3.
2. Concurrently with Tocqueville, in 1838, James Fenimore Cooper was writing, "Equality, in a social sense, may be divided into that of condition, and that of rights. Equality of condition is incompatible with civilization, and is found only to exist in those communities that are but slightly removed from the savage state. In practice, it can only mean a common misery." James Fenimore Cooper, *The American Democrat* (1838; reprint, New York: Alfred A. Knopf, 1931), p. 45.
3. The constitution of France tries to obviate this possibility, by prescribing, in Article 89, "The republican form of government shall not be the object of an amendment." But what is to prevent the nation of France from amending its constitution to abolish Article 89?
4. Tocqueville, *Democracy in America,* p. 5.
5. In Eastern Europe, where such associations have come to be known collectively as "civil society," they played a considerable role in bringing about the revolutions of 1989. The lesson of Tocqueville is that the greatest task of East Europe's civil societies may lie ahead: preventing the democratic state from intruding into private spheres.
6. In 1935, Sinclair Lewis published a striking novel depicting how a very American fuehrer, might come to power during the decade of dictators. See Sinclair Lewis, *It Can't Happen Here* (New York: New American Library, 1970).
7. Tocqueville, *Democracy in America,* vol. 1, p. 208.

6

Tocqueville and Marx

Karl Marx was an intellectual of bourgeois origin. Like most intellectuals of his time and social milieu, he was a revolutionary. The University of Berlin that he attended was hostile to the conservatism of the Prussian state. In religious matters, he was a free thinker and, though he would have disavowed this distinction, a follower of the philosopher Georg Hegel.

As an avowed materialist, Marx homed in on the changes occurring in the industrial societies, notably the British, French, and Prussian. Not so surprisingly, he found that the data of his investigation validated his philosophical assumptions and, hence, sustained his philosophical system. Not so surprisingly, too, he capped this philosophical construct with a Utopian vision: the class conflict would be transcended and communist society would live at peace with itself.

Tocqueville, an aristocrat by birth and a liberal by intellectual formation, was concerned with the preservation of moral and spiritual values in democratic societies. His thought, skeptical and realist, lacked the sheen of utopian fervor. Thus, Marx thought of himself as an economist and a revolutionary. Tocqueville did not claim to be the former, and, as for the latter, he both viscerally abhorred and philosophically rejected revolution as the mainspring of social change.

For Tocqueville, the abolition of hereditary inequalities and the establishment of equality before the law were the heart of the matter, legal inequalities having been the principal cause of social conflicts that, in the past, had led to revolution and civil war. With these legal inequalities removed, Tocqueville argued, passage from the old order to the new could be made without violence; indeed, it was in the nature of democracy to seek fundamental change by peaceable deliberation rather than violent confrontation.

Having resolved the issue of equality, an essentially political issue, men would proceed to devote their energies to economic enterprise and savor its fruits. Hence, in democratic societies, it would be economic interests that overrode all others.

In this sense, we may say, an awareness of commerce as the coming era's dominant force is the point where Marx and Tocqueville meet. If, proceeding from this point, the two philosophies—Tocqueville's liberalism and Marx' socialism—had cultivated their common ground, a Hundred Years' War over ideology need not have been fought. In the event, however, Marx's insistence on the irreconcilable struggle between the classes as the necessary step to the formation of modern society carried the day.

The history of Western democracy shows, first, that this step was not necessary, and, second, that it was a disaster for those who took it. In their Manifesto of 1847, Karl Marx and Friedrich Engels called upon the workers of the world to cast off their chains. Their message has been fulfilled: ever since Tocqueville and Marx wrote their great books, general affluence has advanced with giant strides in all industrial societies. Throughout the lands of Western democracy, the working men and women of the industrialized countries have successfully resisted their "immiseration," and the rise of average wages and standards of living have confounded Karl Marx's baleful prophecies. Globally, though the realm of inequality and want is still desperately large, it has been shrinking—as Tocqueville foresaw and Marx deemed impossible. The notable exceptions to these trends, of course, have been the countries that purport to have adopted the Marxist model.[1]

Now, refighting old ideological battles is a singularly unrewarding occupation, and pure socialism (like pure capitalism) can be found only in the dusty attics of academia and in the rhetoric of the rulers of those wretched Third World countries that cannot afford to practice either. Yet, the great ideologies, battered and bruised by events as they might be, are still with us. They refuse to die. The issues that they address and that are the reason of their existence are often said to have vanished, having been resolved, or having lost their urgency. But then they reappear, reawakened by changes in the balance of social-political forces for which existing institutions do not allow sufficient scope for adjustment.

So it is with the great ideological clash here personified by Tocqueville and Marx. The former maintained that the first step towards freedom under law is the establishment of equality before the law. Men and women, equal before the bar of justice, begin to enact legislation and, thus, to govern themselves. That is not mere theory; it is a history of the United States to the present day, despite a deafening rhetoric to the contrary. Whether Americans will be able to continue governing themselves in the future depends on their ability to maintain the balance between the claims of liberty and those of equality. These two principles are adversaries, and it is the chief task of good government to keep this adversarial relationship within bounds, such as those staked out by the American Constitution.

That is the wisdom that Tocqueville possessed and Marx did not: both men agreed that the government of the modern industrial society would be democratic. Both agreed that the trend of history was towards equality of condition. But Tocqueville, who did not feel comfortable with utopias and utopian politicians, was less certain than Marx about democratic society and whether it would live at peace with itself. In the impossible interview, Tocqueville would have said: "Democratic society, certainly; but it could be a tyranny, or it could be liberal. It is up to us."[2] What he actually said was this:

> I am aware that many of my contemporaries maintain that nations are never their own masters here below, and that they necessarily obey some insurmountable and unintelligent power, arising from anterior events, from their race, or from the soil and climate of their country. Such principles are false and cowardly; such principles can never produce aught but feeble men and pusillanimous nations. Providence has not created mankind entirely independent or entirely free. It is true, that around every man a fatal circle is traced, beyond which he cannot pass; but within the wide verge of that circle he is powerful and free: as it is with man, so with communities. The nations of our time cannot prevent the conditions of men from becoming equal; but it depends upon themselves whether the principle of equality is to lead them to servitude or freedom, to knowledge or barbarism, to prosperity or wretchedness.[3]

Marxism, of course, takes the opposite approach: let equality reign though the heavens fall. Indeed, Marx's most enduring, though unintended, contribution to politics has been to provide envy with a scientific justification and, hence, with respectability. Is that a contribution he would embrace today?

Marx never shed his dogmatic blinkers; he was proud of them. He did not foresee the shift of the ideological thrust that the increasing affluence and political power of the masses were to impart to politics.

Tocqueville, rooted intellectually in the eighteenth century and a dispassionate observer of the workings of the first popular democracy in history, now appears to have been more prescient about things to come in politics, national and international.

Were he alive today, Marx could not help but note that, ever since the First World War, forces other than the economics of capitalism have been blocking the view of his promised land. A vigorous empiricist, Marx could be relied upon to see and to cavil at the deviations of contemporary social development from the projections of *Das Kapital.*

Marx was a brilliant borrower of other men's ideas. Were he alive today and, thus, able to perceive how wrong *Das Kapital* has been in predicting the "immiseration" of the proletariat and, come the revolution, the "withering away of the State," he would, without scruple, make Tocqueville's proposition his own: a society that embraces equality as its ruling norm does so to the detriment of its freedoms.

Thus, Marx redivivus would now be at work on a book entitled *Der Egalitarianismus.* In anticipation of the book's completion, he would, by now, have issued a prefatory manifesto calling upon the peoples of the world to cast off the chains of egalitarianism—chains far stronger and more insidious than those that the nineteenth century had loaded upon the working man.

Is this hypothesis about the likely evolution of Marx's thought implausible? Of course, it is not: having first embraced Hegelianism, Marx "stood Hegel on his head," and quarried from the philosopher's idealist system the building blocks of his own materialist system. There is no reason in logic or psychology for assuming that a Marx redivivus would not be capable of "standing himself on his head."

Notes

1. Though they arrived at opposite conclusions, both Tocqueville and Marx failed to give the demographic factor its proper weight. Malthus did—for the wrong reason. See Thomas Malthus, *An Essay on the Principle of Population: Or, a View of Its Past and Present Effects on Human Happiness: With an Inquiry into Our Prospects Respecting the Future Removal or Mitigation of the Evils Which it Occasions* (London: John Murray, 1817).
2. Raymond Aron, "Tocqueville and Marx," *18 Lectures on Industrial Society* (London: Weidenfeld and Nicolson, 1967), ch. 2, pp. 31–43.
3. Alexis de Tocqueville, *Democracy in America,* vol. 2, ed. Phillips Bradley (New York: Vintage Books, 1945), p. 352.

Part II

7

Equality and Egalitarianism

There is little in Tocqueville's writings that spells out his understanding of the relationship of economics to politics. The universe of his political ideas is circumscribed by classical political philosophy.

Aristotle had followed and modified Plato's classification of political systems. He had defined the share of power, and hence the degree of freedom, that each allowed to men under their respective writs. Not being a bold innovator, Tocqueville contented himself with applying the Aristotelian criteria to his analysis of contemporary political society.

Sticking to these criteria, he found that the dilemma of his age was the same as it had long been: man's ancient struggle for order and freedom. Men cannot enjoy freedom in a society that denies their birthright to equality; they cannot enjoy freedom in a society that does not acknowledge differences in their endowments and, hence, that does not allow for inequality. A society that makes equality its ruling norm, does so at the expense of individual freedom. Between the absolutes of freedom and equality, there is room for diverse mixes, approximating the one or the other extreme.

There have been moments when men believed they stood on middle ground—mostly historical epochs of low ideological intensity. But these moments have been few and far between, and the present is not one of them. If anything is clear about the political developments of the twentieth century, it is that we have not struck a stable balance between the primordial alternatives of man's condition in society. For some time, as Tocqueville warned, the balance has been tipping inexorably towards the egalitarian absolute.

By contrast, the Founders thought of themselves, first and foremost, as the guardians of freedom. All men are created equal, said the Declaration of Independence. Thus, only those laws are just that hold equally for all men. And only the society that lives by this truth is a just society. As Tocqueville observed:

> The very next notion …which presents itself to the minds of men in the ages of equality is the notion of uniformity of legislation. As every man sees that he differs but little from those about him, he cannot understand why a rule that is applicable to one man should not be equally applicable to all others.[1]

But these rules applicable to all laws should allow for a citizen's rise, through the exercise of prudence, to a place of eminence and affluence— that is, they allowed for the explicit inequality of citizens. Opportunity beckoned all; fortune smiled upon the excellent few. It is only in this sense that the Founders were egalitarian. Any other notion of equality would have been abhorrent to them. Indeed, the ostentatious *Gleichmacherei* of the Jacobins was not the least among the excesses that estranged American public opinion from revolutionary France.

The point cannot be stated too often, for it tends to slip away and become a chimera. The only true equality is equality before the law; every other form of equality is a snare and a delusion.

Equality of condition, whether absolute or relative, is simply not a desideratum for those who reject egalitarianism. Equality of opportunity is a misguided attempt to satisfy the egalitarians' demand for "social justice," which should be rejected outright. Those who espouse "equality of opportunity" accept the egalitarian belief that differences must somehow be justified. Collectivists, such as John Rawls, say they are justified only if they serve the public interest. Conservatives, such as Irving Kristol, say that differences are justified only if they have been "earned." As the metaphor of the horse race will have it, every citizen starts off equal and all advancement is due to his own efforts.

But this is an impossibility. People do not "start equal" in their physical, intellectual, emotional, or psychological endowments, and there is no reason why they should start equal in their quests for wealth. Contrary to Marxist claims, the quality of life in a free society is not measured by capital accumulation. It is measured by the degree to which one pursues a rationally productive life. Indeed, there is a bit of folk wisdom, not wholly wrong, that suggests that the inheritance of great wealth tends to undermine a person's motivation to lead a rationally productive life.

To put the matter another way: the Founders did not conceive of all men as being socially ranked along a single dimension, measured by a single standard, whether money or orders of nobility. In a free society, all men are free to aspire, within the bounds of their endowments, not only to whatever height they can reach but to whatever they conceive to be the good life—whether that is the life of material achievement or spiritual fulfillment or, simply, the enjoyment of the day without thought of the morrow.

From these propositions, the Founders' drew their most important political conclusions: just as every man is free to choose his own path to self-fulfillment, so he is free to choose only his own. As man is an end in himself, so he is an end only for himself. The task of reaching his goals must burden no one else, and the rewards of his striving must be inalienably his. The task of the state is to keep the path open and the traffic upon it orderly; to insure the security of the realm; and to do all that at the lowest possible charge on the legitimate rewards of each citizen's striving for self-fulfillment.

This is the sum and substance of society's promise of equality to all men living under its writ. It is not a promise of equal means for each of them. Men are not equally endowed with gifts of mind and body, of innate intelligence, character and vitality, and it is not the job of the state to compensate for such differences. Nor is it the job of the state to compensate for the workings of chance and accident. Hence, properly used, equality of opportunity can mean only an equal opportunity to do what one can with what one has. For the Founding Fathers, it was not the starting point nor the ending point of life that mattered, but the process of living—and that is what the right to pursue happiness protected.

Yet starting points and ending points are precisely what matter to egalitarianism: to equalize outcomes as well as opportunities—and to level down as well as up. The egalitarian politician, be he ever so neatly garbed in the robe of Marxist theory, appeals to the crudest, most atavistic, most joyless of the passions that motivate man-in-society: envy. No longer does he claim to plead for the distribution of a surplus that the capitalist class has somehow expropriated from true producers; rather, he calls upon the state to take away wealth whenever it rises above a bare minimum—in the name of "fairness"—and, thus, to remove whatever social privileges wealth might confer upon its possessors. In this process of equalization, there may be some redistribution of wealth. But the true expectation of egalitarians is not so much that the poor shall have an increased share in the nation's wealth as that everbody's share shall be at one and the same level.

Thus, the egalitarian appeal is both negative and static; it is directed at dividing the pie into equal slices; there is no place in it for making the pie larger. In this way, the politics of egalitarianism are even less hospitable than were those of orthodox Marxist socialism towards economic productivity, creative innovation, special skills, and the uncommon qualities of management.

No wonder, then, that economists—non-Marxist as well as Marxist—have failed to adduce statistics showing that mere spoilation of the richer classes accrues to the benefit of the poorer ones. On the contrary, the statistics point in the other direction. In countries that are relatively free economically, a progressive increase in productivity has raised the average standard of living *and* enriched the producers, employers, and workers alike. This correlation has, at times, been very close. At other times, it has been not so close—especially in times of economic recession and international upheaval. But, over the last hundred years, the linkage of capitalist productivity and general welfare has been unbroken: the rich might have gotten richer, but the masses, far from getting poorer, have possessed themselves of a good many, if not most, of the chattels—from cars to labor-saving home appliances to sport to travel— that formerly were reserved for the rich. In many areas of consumption—as, for example, dress, diet, cosmetics, and entertainment—it has become almost impossible to distinguish between the customs of the higher and lower income groups.

Thus, there is a strong case to be made for the contention that Western capitalism has been "levelling up" and not "levelling down." Could it be that, at the end of his life, Marx suspected as much? That is a question for biographers, but it is a fancy of mine to imagine that he did suspect it. I like to imagine that Marx, a diligent enough empiricist in his own bookish way, discerned the complications that this phenomenon— the enrichment of the "proletarian"—was introducing into his theory and, thus perplexed, left *Das Kapital* unfinished.[2]

Notes

1. Alexis de Tocqueville, *Democracy in America,* vol. 2, ed. Phillips Bradley (New York: Vintage Books, 1945), p. 306.
2. Marx, who died in 1883, worked on volumes 2 and 3 of *Das Kapital* to the end of his life; Friedrich Engels arranged to have them published in 1885 and 1894 respectively.

8

The Hypocrisies of Egalitarianism

The phenomena denoted by the terms "neo-Marxist," "neo-social-ist," "paternalist," and "populist" encode political tendencies that converge in one broad political movement: the surge of egalitarianism. Like all political ideologies, egalitarianism pretends to aspire to the making of a better society—a society free not only from want but also of class barriers that hinder access to education, jobs, and, in general, a fulfilling life. Is the condemnation of egalitarianism as a nefarious political doctrine and of the egalitarian state as a political monstrosity synonymous with condemning the goals that it pretends to seek? Of course, it is not. What is condemned are the pretenses—the institutionalized hypocrisies—of egalitarianism that frustrate the achievement of its avowed objectives. Three such hypocrisies are examined here: the hypocrisies of equality, solvency, and democracy.

The Hypocrisy of Equality

If it has been the purpose of socialism-in-power to dismantle the class structure, and to establish an order of universal equality, then its exertions have failed. In fact, it has riveted on the peoples under its rule hierarchies more complex, powerful, and irremovable than those evolved by feudalism; and it has fostered a pretense of solvency despite chronic insolvency.

Wherever it has come to power, socialism has substituted for the capitalist system and its social order privileges as intricately graded and as sharply differentiated as those enjoyed by the ruling classes of monarchies. Without scruple, the socialist state distributes to its high officialdom perquisites that we might call "egalitarian inequalities." That these perquisites are claimed as the proper attributes of diligent public service;

that they are paid for out of taxation levied upon the populace, and not out of individual income; and that they are supposed to be under legislative review, all this does not diminish their desirability, savor, and costliness. Nor does it alter their significance: whoever, under socialism, wishes to rise above the mass of men, duly equalized in the name of egalitarianism, needs to assume its leadership. Indeed, to hold power under socialism is in itself, and without benefits of any attendant perquisites, a fervently sought distinction that the power holder does not share with the ruled, however "equal" they might be to him socially and economically.[1]

Thus, the avowed ethos of egalitarianism tries the egalitarian power holder's sensitivity to the paradox of a ruling class in a classless society. The egalitarian leader's lifestyle—dress, turn-of-phrase, recreational pursuits, conviviality—need to cleave closely to the lifestyle of his mass following, at least when circumstances expose him to public view. Some egalitarian leaders, past and present, have led lives of exemplary commonness, down to discarding the accoutrements that, once upon a time, graced the lifestyle of the upper and upper-middle classes. That does not mean, however, that they have spurned the perquisites of office that endow them with amenities as uncommon and as costly as—if not more costly than—those at the bidding of great private wealth. This cornucopia of official perquisites contains such entitlements as spacious residences, amply staffed; fleets of planes, helicopters, and limousines; and a retinue of aides ministering to the personal needs of the office holder and his family. Thus, the socialist rulers of the classless Soviet Union, perhaps more self-assured about egalitarianism-in-office than their Western colleagues, never appeared before their people coatless or tieless, and resided behind high, well-guarded walls.

Not surprisingly, the lesser hierarchs—the high bureaucrats—of the egalitarian state manage effortlessly to adapt themselves to the behavior at the summit. They, too, pay homage to that lifestyle of the great mass of people that they perceive as undifferentiated, hence popular, hence "democratic"—hence equal. But they, too, enjoy—and possessively clutch—the graded perks of rank and office. In most Western lands under socialism, they do so discreetly, for in a state that is supposed to be, by ideological definition, classless, discretion must govern the conduct of a ruling class.

Of course, every system of political rule contains a measure of hypocrisy. The reason for this lies in the relationship between the rulers and the ruled, the few that hold power and the many that are held by it. All political systems seek to legitimize this relationship by vesting the power of ruling and the purpose of ruling with moral sanction: the divine right of kings, the mantra of the aristocracy, and the will of the people, in the first instance; the common good, in the second. Only in this way, according to the Greek and Roman philosophers, was government to be justified. Any ruler—monarch, aristocracy, or people—that ruled in his own interests was by definition evil—tyrant, oligarchy, or mob.

Thus, a ruler, desirous of perpetuating his rule, must cite such principles as the sanction for his rule. He cannot concede that he seeks power to satisfy his own wants and to possess himself of privileges that are denied to the ruled. He needs to behave as if he exercises power in the interest of the ruled, that even a government not by the people is a government for the people—or, at least, for a good many of them. In short, he must elevate his pursuit of power to an impersonal principle that is as binding on the ruler as on the populace, for only in this way can government keep at bay the inherent propensity of man to cavil at the restraints imposed upon him by other men, and to cast off the bondage of authority. If there is any constant in political history, it is this propensity to revolt.

But though a divergence between private motive and public sanction exists in every political system, the form and degree of this hypocrisy endemic to political rule varies from one political system to another. In some, there is no need for the ruler to keep the reality and the trappings of his power from public view: indeed, the very show of lordly pomp and circumstance serves to divert, delight, or awe the ruled. In other systems, the power and wealth of the ruling class are sanctioned by institutional ethics—the just rewards of godliness, wisdom, patriotism, or simply hard work.

The apologists of egalitarianism, however, face a peculiarly difficult task in this regard. Advocates of a free society, for instance, may invoke an invisible hand, as in economics, and admit that men are lured to seek power for private reasons but that they are impelled, *volens nolens,* to exercise power in the public interest by structural constraints. They can thus allow for the existence of power's perquisites.

The rhetoric of the egalitarian, however, appeals in the name of social justice and distributive economics to the all-dissolving acid of envy—envy of all distinctions by which one person may be elevated over another. In an egalitarian society, therefore, it behooves the citizen not to flaunt what might be taken by others as perquisites of office.

A similar problem has beset socialism economically. The heroic figure of orthodox socialism was the worker: collectively, the proletariat. But under the influence of egaliatarianism, neo-socialist ideology has been forced to discard the worker in favor of the "disadvantaged," that is, all those who think of themselves as being deprived of access to achievement—and as being deprived forever unless the state, by its bounty, remedies their respective disadvantages.

In Europe, not a few working men—the rank and file of socialism—have noted the ideological shift. They frown upon the rise of a neo-Marxism that is populist rather than socialist and that appeals to what traditional Marxism has always deemed a non-class—and which, by any sociological definition, is not a social class. At the heart of this neo-Marxist doctrine—that Marx would have execrated as the apotheosis of the *Lumpenproletariat* (the proletariat of the derelicts)—lies the notion that the condition of the "disadvantaged" is structural, and that only the state can alter it to his advantage.[2] This idea legitimizes a state that is paternalist rather than socialist.

The Hypocrisy of Solvency

State paternalism and state bureaucracy are synonyms, for the wants of the disadvantaged are countless, and each identified want requires specialized care—*ad infinitum*. Of course, bureaucrats are, whatever else, not disadvantaged. In social space, the perspectives of the bureaucracy of the paternalist state is downward looking. Yet the logic of paternalism requires that the advantaged bureaucrat win the approbation of his disadvantaged clientele and, at least in appearance, identify himself with it.

This condition at the base of the state percolates upward to its top, for the men at the top owe their high places to the votes at the base—the votes of the disadvantaged and the ever-increasing number of their bureaucratic servants. It is in the interests of the latter that the pool of the disadvantaged shall not run dry. It needs to be fed by ever-increasing freshets and rivulets of new claims: if one clientele no longer requires the providential care of the state, another one has to be found to replace it. The congenital tendency of bureaucracy to proliferate—a process akin to amoebic mitosis—does the rest to maintain its growth. Hence, the chronic insolvency of the paternalist state.

Now, the resources of even the richest state, available for the satisfaction of the claims on its bounty, are limited. Moreover, the demands stimulated by the state itself always increase faster and grow more costly than foreseen—and nearly always exceed the budgetary estimates presented to the electorate and its representatives.

For better or worse, however, states do not go bankrupt. They discharge obligations that would force a private business into liquidation by the manipulation of the instruments of fiscal and monetary policy that are the exclusive possession of sovereign power. It is this use of the state's sovereign power that is the source—the one and only source—of that degradation that befalls the state's legal tender. The addiction of the paternalist state to inflation is thus as chronic as that to overspending.

If the economic history of this century has taught one lesson it is that chronic inflation disadvantages more people than it profits; that it erodes confidence in public authority; that it levies on society as a whole indiscriminate and undeclared tribute; and that its social consequences, though they might be slow in coming, are as far reaching as are the effects of those violent upheavals that the scale of history records as political revolutions.

It follows that, if the majority of the populace were fully cognizant of the inflationary process, they would put an end to it, and that their electoral strength would force the paternalist state to measure its bounty to its real rather than its fictitious resources. If the paternalist state has succeeded in postponing this day of reckoning, it has done so by invoking the authority of economic theories that vest its practice with scientific respectability, or, while conceding some of the more obvious blemishes of institutionalized profligacy, advocate the acceptance of this condition as the price that modern society pays for social peace.

These theories view the practice of the paternalist state as either innocuously reasonable or reasonably innocuous. Their gist can be reduced to two propositions that, though they are inconsistent with one another, can be found in many an apology for the exactions of the paternalist state: a) deficits and inflationary policies are economically necessary to invigorate the national economy ("prime the pump"), the costs of this remedial treatment being offset by future growth; or b) they are politically necessary to ward off the disruptive threat to society as a whole posed by the restiveness of its disadvantaged part.

Since neither of these apologies can in fact ward off chronic insolvency, the pretense of solvency, concurrent with the deliberate stimulation of popular demands that can be met only out of the public exchequer, is as integral to the politics of egalitarianism as is the egalitarian cant of the ruling class. Both these conceits are necessary for the sustenance of the modern paternalist state. Both conform exactly to the classic definition of hypocrisy: the practice of feigning to be what one is not. Egalitarianism does exactly that.

The Paradox of Democracy

In one important respect, the politics of egalitarianism does not differ from any other: the politician's purpose is always to control people—to rule. Thus, the egalitarian politician, like any other politician, seeks to bend the popular will to his purpose, in short, to impose *his* will upon the populace. Insofar as he succeeds in this purpose he will have created a new social order, for whatever the social norms mandated by the popular will, that norm cannot be his. If it were, he would have to surrender his hard-won power to uncontrolled anarchy. No politician in power has ever been an anarchist.

Now, it can be argued that all political ideologies are so many fig leaves for the will to power, but, among these emblems of modesty, the one that is supposed to hide the extremity of egalitarianism is least deceptive. The central axiom of egalitarianism, namely, the reduction of all social hierarchies to a common norm mandated by the popular will, elevates iconoclastic atavism to the creative principle of social order. But all we need to do in order to strip off the cant of this axiom is to ask three questions:

1. Who will define the criteria of proper social equality?
2. Who will mandate the proper social equality?
3. Who will adjudicate and administer the application of the criteria of proper social equality?

The first two of these three questions are in fact unanswerable within the premises of egalitarianism. Practically, socialism-in-power has always required the antecedent existence of a political elite guiding the popular will towards a state of equality, that state of equality that satisfies the criteria established by none other than the same political elite. As for the third question: obviously, it cannot be answered without conceding the existence of a political class empowered to administer the classless social order, that is, to see to it that deviations from the common norm do not occur—and that the order thus created will sustain itself. Thus, each of these questions begs an answer that reduces the egalitarian axiom to an absurdity.

Notes

1. This is a truth that, as the classical philosophers knew, holds *mutatis mutandis* under any political system. It explains why capitalists have been known to prefer using great wealth as a means to power, rather than for personal comfort or the creation of additional wealth: witness the enormous sums spent by wealthy individuals to win popular election.

2. *Lumpenproletariat* (German, *Lumpen* (rag) + proletariat, "detestable proletariat"): "According to Karl Marx in *The Communist Manifesto*, [the *Lumpenproletariat*] is the lowest stratum of industrial working class, including also such undesirables as tramps and ciminals. The members of the *Lumpenproletariat*—'this social scum,' said Marx—are not only disinclined to participate in revolutionary activities with their 'rightful brethren,' the proletariat, but also tend to act as the 'bribed tools of reactionary intrigue.'" *The New Encyclopaedia Britannica*, s.v. "Lumpenproletariat."

9

Meritocracy

Sophistry is the compliment that absurdity pays to reason. Thus, it should not surprise anyone that, in this age of intellectual confusion, egalitarianism has found it easy to recruit subtle apologists who can translate crude appeals to envy into a system of lofty public ethics.[1] These obliging thinkers, though shunning the gross simplifications of populism, have been hard at work garbing populism in the dress of meritocracy, in order that it might make its debut in the drawing rooms of intellectual sophistication.

But, what, we may ask, has meritocracy to do with equality? Are not the two concepts mutually exclusive? Paradoxically, they are not, and indeed the most popular (as well as the best-selling) statements of egalitarian philosophy now cluster around the idea of meritocratic rule.

Common to these statements of egalitarianism are three ideas: the egalitarian idea that any hierarchy not based on merit is both unjust and inefficient; the utilitarian idea that merit is measured by the contribution an individual makes to society; and the elitist idea that such a contribution can be assessed by the hierarchy of the meritorious.

Meritocracy and Bureaucracy

The usefulness of this logic is hard to exaggerate. Contrary to Marx's prognosis, the state—be it socialist in name as it was in the communist dominions, be it under socialist management as in some Western countries—has refused to "wither away," and proliferating bureaucracies of power seekers have penetrated into the terrain evacuated by bourgeois capitalism.

In this context, the concept of a meritocracy serves to bring Marxism up to date: it pretends to reconcile Marx's egalitarian ethics with some calculus of social cost-effectiveness.[2] And it satisfies the power hunger of the post-capitalist elite: first, by allowing them to define the concept of merit; and secondly, by giving them the authority to implement its application to social hierarchies.

If so blatant a grab for power were made by a man on horseback, the American people would rise up spontaneously and turn back the threat. That the American people cannot see the equivalent threat posed by a meritocratic elite we owe to the ahistorical—or, rather, the anti-historical—teachings of what passes as modern, progressive education, which have gone far in erasing the memory of the people. Insisting upon the uniqueness of the contemporary human condition—do we not live in an unprecedented "technotronic age?"—this egalitarian pedagogy rejects the relevance of historical analogy.

Yet, the idea of a meritocracy—to wit, an all-powerful bureaucracy issued from, and administering in perpetuity, a system of merit—is at least as old as the temples of Greece and the Great Wall of China: its most celebrated theoretical formulation was the rule of Plato's philosopher kings; its most notorious realization was the Mandarin rule of Imperial China.[3] If, therefore, the Open Society perishes, it will be because of a lapse of its historical memory—because it can no longer recognize its oldest foe when it sees him.

The Structure of Meritocracy

Defining the structure of a meritocratic society raises problems exactly like the problems raised by the egalitarian norm. Is there such thing as an objective standard of civic meritoriousness, not to speak of meritoriousness in the arts, or the sciences? If there is, how and by whom will the standard of what is and is not meritorious be determined? How and by whom will the system of merit then be administered and perpetuated?

Historically, the answer to the latter two questions has been: a body of meritorious men (and sometimes women as well) will perform these tasks. If this is to be the answer, then how will that body renew itself? And what will happen to those who, because of age, illness, or other reasons, cease to be meritorious? Will they be eliminated by the consensus of their peers, in the formation of which consensus they themselves participate?

Anybody familiar with the proceedings of the world's most prestigious bodies dedicated to the spotting and rewarding of merit—from the Nobel Committees, to the French Academy, on to countless professional selection boards—will doubt not necessarily the worth of their contribution to the maintenance of professional standards and the collegiate *esprit de corps* but certainly their infallibility.

If the important scientific and artistic innovations of the last hundred years had had to wait for the recognition of expert committees before launching themselves upon their creative undertakings, then, in all likelihood, men would still be bound to this earth rather than soaring into space, and the creative arts would still be shackled to academic rote.[4] There has never been, and there cannot be, a creativity certified by committee. Indeed, though this might seem an argument for meritocracy, we might wonder what would have happened to Karl Marx if the scientific merit of *Das Kapital* and the civic meritoriousness of its publication had been subject to the determination of the economists of his day.

Freedom versus Meritocracy

The open society does not perform tidily, and its untidiness—its large number of failures for each success; its openness to unexpected and unforeseeable entries into the competition—has always been displeasing to the advocates of centralized state power and the all-powerful, all-knowing planner. So, too, has the open society's lack of elitism been displeasing to elites. In a free society, the merit of an achievement is what the open market says it is.[5]

By contrast, societies run by state bureaucracies, such as those of the defunct Soviet Union and its dependencies, are if nothing else more tidy than ours: bureaucrats determine in advance what will have merit and what will not, sparing society the cost of wasteful failures and uneducated judgment.

No wonder, then, that the intellectual vanguard of the paternalist state has devoted so much energy to denying one fact: the openness of Western society, the diffusion of its private associations, the wide range of alternatives that it offers to imagination and enterprise, the latitude it affords to dissent, its tolerance of error, and, above all, its distrust of institutionalized omniscience, has fostered an unprecedented flowering of talents and unleashed the greatest surge of creativity in history.

By contrast, the evidence available to date tells us that the great social-ist bureaucracies have reduced great peoples, as richly endowed with natural wealth and human resources as are the Western democracies, to a cultural wasteland and, but for the materiel of war, to economic stag-nation. If published statistics are not misleading, then that stagnation would long ago have given way to a state of downright retrogression, had it not been for the input, mostly unrequited, of capitalist goods, material and intellectual.

The Soviet Union elevated to ruling dogma the principles of meritoc-racy, this peerless system of advancement, this austere, incorruptible, and efficient bureaucracy, renewing itself from an ever-flowing source of equality of opportunity. Here, the Soviet rulers proclaimed, was the fulfillment of Marx's promise that, under socialism, everyone would be able to produce according to his abilities and everyone would partake of the product only according to his needs.

Thus was a system of advancement by merit, rather than by the privi-lege of birth or personal favor or financial advantage, vested with the unchallengeable authority of the all-powerful state, and thus was it re-ceived without audible dissent by the acclaim of all domestic media of information. It was presented to the universe as the proudest achieve-ment of socialist development.

Under the circumstances, we are entitled to learn from glasnost how such a system worked in practice. Not so surprisingly, we find, the light of utopian socialism had failed, and failed signally, in the corridors of bureaucratic power. The bureaucracy of the Soviet state, responsible to no one but itself, renewed its membership by nepotism, intrigue, and, at the top, not infrequently by the use of naked force, including murder. Moreover, if the condition of the average Soviet man—his pay, diet, and housing—provide a measure of administrative efficiency, then the So-viet bureaucracy proved itself massively incompetent in all sectors of civic interest, except the organs of repression.

Notes

1. A most notable example is John Rawls, *Theory of Justice* (Cambridge, Mass.: Harvard University, 1971).
2. See Michael Young, *The Rise of the Meritocracy* (London, 1958).
3. "Unless, said I, either philosophers becomes kings in our states or those whom we now call our kings and rulers take to the pursuit of philosophy seriously and

adequately, and there is a conjunction of these two things, political power and philosophical intelligence...there can be no cessation of troubles, dear Glaucon." book V, 473 b-e, *The Republic,* trans. Paul Shorey, in Plato, *The Collected Dialogues,* ed. Edith Hamilton and Huntington Cairns (Princeton, N.J.: Princeton University Press, 1961), pp. 712-13.

"Many centuries passed, however, before the idea of government through bureaucracy, selected on the basis of learning, reached its fulfillment. Not until the T'ang dynasty (AD 618-907) was the examination system, through which the mandarins were selected, functioning fully." *The New Encyclopaedia Britannica,* s.v. "Asia."

4. Rocket pioneer Robert Goddard was dismissed by his contemporaries as "a sort of crackpot." Walter A. McDougall, *The Heavens and the Earth: A Political History of the Space Age* (New York: Basic Books, 1985), p. 77. T.S. Eliot's "The Love Song of J. Alfred Prufrock," now considered the first masterpiece of modernist poetry, languished at *Poetry* for more than a year while the editor, Harriett Monroe, tried to decide if it was poetry.

5. "As a matter of fact, capitalism at its apogee saw itself as the most just social order the world has ever witnessed, because it replaced all arbitrary (e.g., inherited) distributions of power, privilege, and property with a distribution that was directly and intimately linked to personal merit—this latter term being inclusive of both personal abilities and personal virtues." Irving Kristol, "'When Virtue Loses All Her Loveliness'—Some Reflections on Capitalism and the 'Free Society,'" *Two Cheers for Capitalism* (New York: Mentor, 1979), pp. 244-45.

10

Democracy and Discipline

Today, democracy remains the paradoxical phenomenon that fascinated Tocqueville. Its perpetuity depends, as Tocqueville perceived, not only on the effectiveness of its institutions but, far more, on the vigor of moral forces that issue from religious beliefs and social conventions predating the rise of democratic institutions.

Yet, these ancient beliefs and conventions are now under serious assault—by forces that equality, democracy, and liberty themselves unleash. To take but one example: the free market is a critical bulwark of equality, liberty, and democracy.[1] At the same time, however, it engenders a popular passion for consumption that has been dubbed consumerism. This passion is intensified by increases in the quantity and variety of goods produced for consumption. Its result is to weaken its own foundations, such as the postponement of consumption, which is a necessary element in the creation of both human and financial capital, and in the defense of persons, property, and vital interests. Thus, increased consumption results from liberty, and, at the same time, weakens its base, economically and morally. He who points out this paradox of our society should not expect to be warmly received in either capitalist or anticapitalist circles.

However, unlike certain contemporary conservatives, who share my concern for morality, I am not calling for a return to "religious roots" or saying that we require a religiously guided society. One need not believe in God in order to be a moral man. Some of the greatest good men of the ages did not believe in him. They believed in goodness; and goodness has flowed from them into the hearts of men, be they ever so selfish. Had it been otherwise, Plato could not have filtered his philosophy from that moral man, Socrates, and the West's greatest scientists, past and present, could not have thought of their ardent pursuit of scientific truth as serving the good of humanity. To be a moral man, so far as we can see from history, what one needs to believe in is some conception of human existence that transcends the fleeting pleasure of the moment. This implies a sense of moral discipline. As Aleksandr I. Solzhenitsyn adumbrates:

> The time is urgently upon us to limit our wants. It is difficult to bring ourselves to sacrifice and self-denial, because in political, public, and private life we have long since dropped the golden key of self-restraint to the ocean floor. But self-limitation is the fundamental and wisest step of a man who has obtained his freedom. It is also the surest path toward its attainment. We must not wait for external events to press harshly upon us or even topple us. Through prudent self-restraint we must learn to accept the inevitable course of events.[2]

Without such a conception, our lives are not only short but also brutish, lacerated by violence, and stifled by ignorance. Western civilization has been blessed by its ability to bring together several transcendent ethics, sacred and secular. And yet we occupy only a small clearing in the primitive jungle from which man can see the sky. There remains a vast region of brutishness beyond our clearing, and nature is still as indifferent to man as it has always been. Perhaps, therefore, the most profound question of contemporary democracy is whether its peoples retain the moral resources to continue clearing the jungle, or even to hold it at bay.

Indefinite Perfectability

Paradoxically, men in the modern West have tended to believe not only that their culture is healthy, but that it is always progressing and will always progress—that the clearing in the jungle is always widening, and that one day all men will be able to see all of the sky.

This idea of progress—infinite and felicitous—is, as history goes, of recent date and, like most of our ideas about man in society, rooted in the thought of the philosophes of the eighteenth-century Enlightenment. It is at the heart and center of Tocqueville's philosophical analysis of American democracy.

The heading of chapter 8 in the first book of volume 2 of *Democracy in America* is: "Equality Suggests to the Americans the Idea of the Indefinite Perfectability of Man." Expanding on the challenge of this hypothesis, Tocqueville wrote as follows:

> Equality suggests to the human mind several ideas which would not have originated from any other source, and it modifies almost all those previously enter-

tained. I take as an example the idea of human perfectability, because it is one of the principal notions that the intellect can conceive, and because it constitutes of itself a great philosophical theory, which is everywhere to be traced by its consequences in the conduct of human affairs.

Although man has many points of resemblance with the brutes, one trait is peculiar to himself,—he improves: they are incapable of improvement. Mankind could not fail to discover this difference from the beginning. The idea of perfectability is therefore as old as the world; equality did not give birth to it, but has imparted to it a new character.[3]

Tocqueville's language is, as always, clear and simple. I cannot think of any statement about the ideas that have driven and still drive American democracy that are as clear and simple as these sentences.

Progress, Permissiveness, and Luck

Man has "improved." American democracy has led the West's greatest defense against "brutishness"—the brutishness of Nazi and Soviet despotism. In its own home, American democracy has striven to still the most raucous voices of unreason and brutality. No one can deny our successes.

And yet the clearing remains small; the brutishness close by; and our democracy's tolerance for pilot error—its ability to withstand the consequences of mistakes—is as narrow as it has ever been. An economic crisis at home or turbulence abroad could release destructive forces now quiescent. For an understanding of this chronic malaise, we must again look to the American character.

Discipline and sacrifice of self are a matter of education. Since the time of Tocqueville, however, American civilization has become increasingly permissive. The authority of traditional figures—pastor, pedagogue, and paterfamilias—has been undermined, in no small part by the consumerism of our democratic society.

With the undermining of authority, the strength of the nation also has been sapped, and where a nation's strength is diminished, necessarily the role of luck increases. In this century, as a result, the democracies' tolerance of pilot error has been narrow—at certain times in their turbulent passage no wider than a hair's breadth.

In the case of World War I, perhaps, we could not have lost it even if the Allied statesmen and their commanders had been less qualified for making war and concluding peace than were the Greys and Haigs, the Poincarés and Lloyd Georges.[4] But World War II, to paraphrase the Duke of Wellington, was a much closer "close-run thing" than the democratic people, flushed with victory, thought it was. Without Hitler's demented assistance, Germany might well have dropped the first nuclear bomb.

The reason has to do with the nature of scientific excellence that has made and re-made Western civilization. Excellence, whether in the sciences or the arts, is achieved only by unstinting labor and self-sacrifice—as exacting and sacrificial as the search for divine truth that drove the founders of great religions. Scientific excellence is a product not only of intellectual genius but also of discipline—severe and unremitting. It is thus a commodity of sufficient rarity that no modern state can safely alienate it.

Yet that is just what Hitler did, by driving Jewish scientists into exile. In World War I, the vast majority of German Jews loyally and proudly served the Kaiser; only the mania of the fuehrer deprived World War II Germany of their contribution to the country's greatest strategic asset: scientific excellence.[5] Thus it happened that most of the nuclear scientists active in the United States in the 1930s and 1940s were born in Germany or Austria-Hungary, and most of them were Jewish by descent.

Notes

1. See "From Containment to Engagement," Remarks of Anthony Lake, assistant to the president for national security affairs, Johns Hopkins University, School of Advanced International Studies, Washington, D.C., September 21, 1993 (typescript), *passim.*
2. Aleksandr I. Solzhenitsyn, "To Tame Savage Capitalism," *The New York Times,* November 28, 1993.
3. Alexis de Tocqueville, *Democracy in America,* vol. 2, ed. Phillips Bradley (New York: Vintage Books, 1945), p. 34.
4. Upon the intervention of the United States, the sheer weight of Allied power was bound to crush Germany. That the Allies, having won the war, lost the peace, for this no one was to blame but the Allies themselves, who, no sooner than the last shot had been fired by the victorious democracies, managed to fall out with one another.
5. The same effect was observable in medicine as well. "The scientific ladder-climbing of immigrants such as [Selman] Waksman [who won the Nobel Prize in Medicine]...demonstrated that in America science would evolve as a meritocracy rather than along old-regime bloodlines. This worked to everyone's advantage in the end, but most particularly as the Nazis forced gifted scientists to flee to the U.S. where they contributed their skills and energies to the effort to cure tuberculosis." Jerome E. Groopman, "How We Beat TB," *The Wall Street Journal,* September 7, 1993.

11

Bureaucracy

In each of the three great wars that dominated the twentieth century, democracy won. On the face of it, these victories seem to close a chapter of history. Democracy has never been as proof against its enemies as it is now.

But will it stay that way?

Ever since the peoples of the Greek city-states chose to govern themselves, the freedom of equals has been the basic principle of the democratic spirit. It is a magnificent principle. With its conception, begins the history of Western civilization, and—as is the fate of all magnificent ideas—its erosion by the forces it set free.

Tocqueville saw this, and warned against it. Perhaps the most admirable and engaging trait of *Democracy in America* is the author's cool objectivity. He is confident in his prognosis: democracy is destined to prevail throughout the globe; it is the best government designed by man— and, so the devout Catholic infers, willed by God. But Tocqueville does not claim for democracy a competence in matters that cannot be dealt with by legislation.

At their best, people are able to govern themselves competently, which means, to choose their governors wisely. But this is all a democracy can do, and all it should do. It cannot add to the rights with which man is endowed by his creator. It can only protect those rights—or violate them.

Increasingly, democracy does the latter, as Tocqueville feared. He had gleaned the universal attraction of the idea of democracy but also its vulnerability to perversion in the name of equality. Thus, he could not still his doubts about the ability of democracy to unite liberty with equality, and this was his tragedy. He asked the right question, but he could not answer it. No one else has answered it either.

Today, we see, powerful interests and their obliging ideologues are proposing that democracy exceed its writ and set the standards of the good life, molding the "Democratic Man for All Seasons." It would be a colossal irony of history if the free peoples, having rid the world of communism, inflicted upon themselves a bondage that resembles too close for comfort what they helped the ex-Soviet peoples to shake off.

Yet that appears to be what they are doing. The slide toward centralized bureaucracy that troubled Tocqueville has accelerated at a stupendous rate. It has buried beneath its files the better part of private life. Tocqueville, who popularized the word "bureaucracy," foresaw the trend; he did not foresee the immensity of its sweep.

Tocqueville, in his day, foresaw that the idea of America would one day defeat the ideas of monarchy and aristocracy. Today, it seems, the creeping bureaucratic centralization of American democracy is the posthumous revenge of bureaucratic-monarchical Europe.

The idea of the centrally administered paternal state has come to America from Europe. It took it about fifty years to transit from Bismark's Berlin to Franklin Roosevelt's Washington, and another fifty to push the nation to the brink of insolvency.[1] During the latter period, this new conception of the state has also been assimilated into the average American's way of thinking about work and its rewards, about individual achievement and the claims of the individual on the collectivity, and about the claims of the collectivity on the individual.

The paternalistic state—Tocqueville's "absolute, minute, regular, provident and mild" master—now seems likely to rule the peoples on both sides of the Atlantic. Is it absolutely unimaginable that, within the not-too-far-off future, the Western democracies will be united in their servitude to conformity rather than the enjoyment of freedom in variety?

I noted earlier that *Democracy in America* was written by a Frenchman for Frenchmen at a critical point of their history. He wrote at a time when the levels of power had passed from the hands of the French aristocracy to those of the bourgeoisie—the bourgeoisie that, in America, had always been in power and, hence, had no revolution to make and no old regime to bury.

Whatever were the uses to which the rulers of France—be they kings, be they military dictators, be they freely chosen representatives—put the power of the states, that power kept on growing. The rulers change, their policies change, the bureaucracy endureth.

Tocqueville did not see the French Revolution as a break in this continuity. To the contrary, the state that emerged from the turmoil of the Revolution and twenty years of Napoleonic Wars was more powerful, more centralized, and more omnipresent than it had been under the crown. The instruments of state power—the police, the educators, and the collectors of taxes—had been honed on the exigencies of war and the preparation for war.

The state grew stronger not only because it ministered to the people's growing needs but also because it made itself feared. Perhaps the most disquieting thing about the paternalistic state is that the more helpless its constituents feel without its care and direction, the more they fear it. Tocqueville could see so far and no further. He did not sketch in the administrative framework that would be likely to enshrine the paternalistic state.

It seems that victorious peoples are prone to adopt the culture of the peoples they defeated. The victorious Romans traded much of their philosophy and virtues for the *douceur de la vie* of the conquered Greeks. The raw Manchus were absorbed almost without a trace by the refined Chinese whom they had conquered.

These reversals suggest an ominous parallel: the communist empire has collapsed into the arms of the democracies, the victors of the cold war. Could communism—no longer encumbered by crude and costly instruments of force, and having rid itself of the image of the global disturber of world peace—not prove a more insidious threat to the freedoms of democracy than its Leninist-Stalinist incarnation? Could Tocqueville's "mild despot" not succeed where the harsh one failed?

At present, this danger seems remote.

For example, if any people should be able to recognize despotism however disguised, the peoples freed from communist rule should. The Soviet Union has been ruled by the most highly centralized bureaucracy in history. The peoples' rejection of communism can be seen as a popular revolt against the centralized bureaucracy, put in place by Lenin and set in blood-stained cement by his successor. Whatever state evolves from the ruins of the Soviet Union, its bureaucratic controls will be looser and less tightly administered from the center than were those of the defunct apparatus. Even allowing for the "worst case"—the total failure of the democratic experiment and the return of collectivism under a fascist label—never again will the ex-Soviet peoples submit to a system of coercion as arbitrary as the Soviet state. Nevertheless, it would be rash to assume that the manifest dissatisfaction of the ex-Soviet peoples with bureaucratic mismanagement has discredited the idea of the paternalistic state in their eyes.

So too in Europe. Socialism, though chastened, still commands the allegiance of about one-half of the voting population. The highly centralized controls of the European welfare states show no signs of loosening. The European states have not relaxed their controls on capitalist enterprise. Countless ties still link private enterprise to the "public sector." Privatization by the grace of the state does not signify the reduction of the state bureaucracy.

The size and the power of the state bureaucracy are the abiding issues of European political debate. No one, however, be he of the Right, be he of the Left, believes that, under any conceivable circumstances, any major political party in Europe will make the reduction in the number of state employees a salient campaign issue. In Europe, the growth of centralized state power seems irreversible. If the scandalous performance of the Soviet bureaucratic apparatus has a lesson to teach, then the European socialists, without whose participation or benevolent neutrality Europe cannot be governed, have not learnt it. To the contrary, in the European countries liberated from communist rule—East Germany and her neighbors—not a few of the leftovers of the communist system of bureaucratic control have been grafted on the organs of the new, the democratic state.

Thus, states throughout the "free world" continue to encroach on the "private sector." As Tocqueville put it in a chapter heading of his *Democracy in America:* "The Opinions of Democratic Nations About Government are Naturally Favorable to the Concentration of Power," and, hence, to the agencies that administer it. There have been periods of rest and even of some retreat. But, over time, and irrespective of the ideological orientation of governments, the advance of state power and its servants has been inexorable: the Majority has willed it so.

The Future of Bureaucracy

As yet, the Western democracies have not altogether given in to the false appeals of egalitarianism. They still cavil at the exactions and growth of their state bureaucracies, executors of the egalitarian mandate.

Their free economic order is, at least in name, still intact: in some countries, only one-third of the national revenue is funnelled through the conduits of the state bureaucracy; in others, one-half is left to the free disposition of the populace—through the workings of the market.

In most Western countries, private associations—professional, educational, charitable, religious, and recreational—still retain the freedom to live by their respective charters, though, in some places, those rights of privacy are precarious and under heavy assault from the levellers.

The basic unit of privacy, the family, still thrives in America, although not, in some places, as vigorously as in the past. So, too, does a passion for liberty. In no other country has the instinctive revulsion against the bureaucratization of the state been more marked and widespread than in the United States; in no other country is the average citizen more resentful of his national and local tax obligations, though, paradoxically, nowhere is he more meticulous in discharging it.

Finally, there is today almost unanimous agreement in America that: 1) the indebtedness of the state is approaching the safe limits of solvency; 2) national budgets, each larger than the previous, contain a lot of undesirable and unnecessary spending; 3) inflation, the consequence of overspending and the concurrent degradation of the currency, is hurting all those who, prudently, have spent less than they earned and have laid up savings for a future of sunny as well as rainy days; and 4) something ought to be done to put a stop to the slide into national bankruptcy and the spoliation of ever-larger sectors of the populace, notably the middle class.

On the face of it, then, one might expect that these noxious trends could be halted by democratic fiat, that legislators responding to constituency pressures would curb the powers of the states and slash budgets. Logical or not, this reversal of fiscal policy has not happened.

Interest Groups

Tocqueville noted the first difficulty faced by the would-be reformer:

It frequently happens that the members of the community promote the influence of the central power without intending to.... Such persons will admit, as a general principle, that the public authority ought not to interfere in private concerns; but, by an exception to that rule, each of them craves its assistance in the particular concern on which he is engaged and seeks to draw upon the influence of the government for his own benefit, although he would restrict it on all other occasions. If a large number of men applies this particular exception to a great variety of different purposes, the sphere of the central power extends itself imperceptibly in all directions, although everyone wishes it to be circumscribed.[2]

It has been the achievement of Western bureaucracies gradually to increase the sense of dependence in their citizenries, so that ever larger numbers of people believe (falsely) that they can not—dare not—engage in any undertaking, including bare survival, without the benefaction of the state. In this way, by the phenomenon Tocqueville observed, the majority that should rise up against its manipulation at the hands of the bureaucracy has been instead turned into a myriad of interest groups.

Interest groups defend their own interests, this being their reason for existence. Some groups defend their interests more successfully than others, and do so to the disadvantage of other interest groups. Some members of these groups understand what is happening and nonetheless believe they can put the fiscal rout, notably the inflationary rampage, to their advantage—thus beating the game. But large numbers of people, who angrily cavil at the costs of the welfare state and other government agencies distributing public monies, are, or expect to be, recipients of public bounty—without seeing any contradiction in their behavior.

As for the possibility that taxpayers might themselves become an interest group, this has proven to be a chimera, except on rare occasions. A person's sense of identity is rarely tied up with his being a taxpayer, except when a particularly onerous or unjust tax has been passed. Consequently, the taxpayer is not often motivated to join groups opposing taxation. On the other hand, a person's sense of identity is frequently tied up with his membership in a group that receives public largesse. The result is that the average citizen is far more likely to join with those of his fellow citizens who seek to expand government largesse than with those who seek to shrink it—and this is the basis of the bureaucracy's power.

The result of this process has been that the take of the bureaucracy, redistributing the taxes collected, and producing nothing except its own increment, has grown at a rate even greater than that of the gross national product and the public debt, a Parkinsonian phenomenon that compounds the absurdity of American people's belief in the great bureaucratic deception.[3]

Notes

1. "Bismarck did not rely only on repression to defeat the Social Democrats. He was the first statesman in Europe to devise a comprehensive scheme of social security, offering the worker insurance against accident [1884—work injury law] sickness [1883-sickness and maternity law] and old age [1889—old age, invalidity, and death law]." *The New Encyclopaedia Brittanica*, s.v. "Bismarck."
2. Alexis de Tocqueville, *Democracy in America*, vol. 2, ed. Phillips Bradley (New York: Vintage Books, 1945), pp. 311-12.
3. In 1900, U.S. governments (at all levels) consumed 8.9 percent of the gross national product; in 1930, 12.2 percent; in 1990, 36.8 percent. In 1992, for the first time, government (at all levels) employed more Americans than manufacturing: 18.2 million versus 18.1 million.

Part III

12

Foreign Policy and Interest Groups

Here, I am not concerned with democracy in America and the changes that, since I first came to America seventy years ago, have profoundly altered American society. Here, I am concerned with the consequences of these changes for America in the world and, hence, the conduct of American foreign policy.

The interplay between domestic and foreign interests determines the making of foreign policy in all countries. This, however, is a matter of degree. In the United States, domestic politics affects foreign policy making more conclusively than in any other country. American foreign policy *is* popular foreign policy. In no other country is the influence of private associations on the conduct of foreign policy as great and as direct as in the United States. In no other country is the debate between the foreign policy maker and his critics, between government and interest groups, between the administration and the opposition more resonant than in the United States.

Lobbies flourish in the capital cities of all democracies. But nowhere are they as well endowed, as confident of their influence on the making of public laws and policies, as unabashed by the ambiguities of their role, as they are in the United States. At the end of the day, it is from the agitation of lobbies that policy rises rather than from the explicit processes of government.

The problem is not the "inefficiency" that lobbies introduce into government. The way in which the structure of government intended by the Founding Fathers has been subverted.

It was among the chief concerns of the Founding Fathers that government should serve national interests rather than private interests. And this was a concern they shared with many other Enlightenment thinkers. It is said that the phrase "the greatest good for the greatest number," before it became the slogan of utilitarians, was Joseph Priestley's protest against the use of the British government for private ends.

At any rate, the Founding Fathers were deeply concerned that "factions" (in their terminology) would direct the policies of government, and sought to avoid that result in two ways. First, through Article I, Section 8, of the Constitution, the Founders sought to limit strictly the functions of government. Today, those limits have been swept away, so that (for example) agricultural lobbies can seek import quotas or export subsidies from the federal government.

The second device of the Founding Fathers, as *The Federalist Papers* explain, was to construct an intricate political/governmental system that would transmute private interests into national interests. Today, most of the intricacies that the Founders built into the constitutional system have also been swept away, so that Congressmen now face vast numbers of voters, whose votes must be garnered by expensive, repetitive mass-media campaigns. And this also opens the door for wealthy lobbies.

Now it remains true that American public opinion is the final maker of American foreign policy, if only because the American lobbyist knows he ultimately must bring the American people around to his viewpoint if he is to secure any sustained foreign policy. A global foreign policy is a costly and risky enterprise; only a few countries can afford global foreign policies of their own, rather than foreign policies that are reactive to the global balance of power but incapable of changing it. Thus, a consensus of public opinion is the precondition for the making of foreign policies that are likely to be very costly and to involve staggering risks. But, sometimes for better, sometimes for worse, public opinion is not the mere summation of private opinions.

Can America, under these conditions, conduct a rational foreign policy? Or do the processes of domestic politics, extended to issues of global politics, prevent American diplomacy from the rational pursuit of national goals?

The question is not an idle one. Its aptness can be illustrated by example.

Exactly seventy years ago to the day of this writing, the Turkish army defeated the Greek army on the plains of Anatolia. The latter, led by King Konstantine in person, had come to take possession of the coastlands of Asia Minor—the Ionia of classic history and homeland of about a million and one-half Greek speakers professing the Greek Orthodox faith.

The time seemed propitious for this venture: the Ottoman Empire, having rashly aligned itself with the loosing side in the Great War, was falling apart. The victorious Allies—Britain and France—had occupied Istanbul (Konstantinopol) and a few choice strategic places on the Asian (Turkish) side of the Straits. In addition, the Allies were sympathetic to the Greeks who, belatedly, had come down on their side. Their military presence at the Bosporus was thought to tie down whatever military forces the Turks had managed to retrieve from the break-up of Ottoman power.

In the summer of 1921, therefore, the Greek army swept into Anatolia and occupied, against little resistance, the most populous and richest part of it. By the criteria of logistics and superiority in armament, the Greeks should have won—Konstantinopol and Smyrna (Istanbul and Izmir) should now be Greek cities.

But it did not turn out that way. The Turkish army, hastily cobbled together and poorly equipped, but led by a man of genius, Mustafa Kemal Pasha, halted the Greek offensive, defeated the Greek army in two major battles, drove it back to the Aegean seaboard—and forced it and hundreds of thousands of Greek civilians to evacuate their ancestral Anatolian home.

The proceedings—as proceedings of this kind always are—were nasty. As always, it was innocent bystanders who bore their brunt. The ensuing peace treaty ratified the result of the massive exchanges of population that were numerically more costly to the Greek side than to the Turkish side. Millions of Greek speakers emigrated from Anatolia to Greece and from Greece to the rest of the world, the preferred and most rewarding goal being the United States.

This arrangement, the Lausanne Treaty, crafted by Allied and Turkish statesmen in 1923, has endured to the present day. It has been neat, though brutal. Since then, Greeks and Turks have not warred upon one another. For seventy years, they have been at peace. They have been several times at the brink of war; diplomacy has saved the day.

Diplomacy, however, has not been able to resolve all the differences among the parties to this Treaty of Peace that—as all peace treaties do—gave to the victor more than to the defeated. The result has been chronically bad Greek-Turkish relations.

Daunting as are the problems posed by this enduring antagonism between the two nation-states, modern Greece and Turkey, they have been burdened by the history of millenarian strife between two cultures, Islam and Christianity. History is what historians make it. Not so surprisingly, Greek historians see Greek-Turkish relations through Greek eyes, just as Turkish historians are apt to see Greek-Turkish relations through Turkish eyes. However, this penchant—though natural and, hence, blameless—has disturbing consequences for the pursuit of American foreign policy.

During this century, many more Greeks than Turks emigrated to the United States—and, for that matter, to Europe. The Greek exodus from Anatolia, enforced by Turkey, increased this disparity. Today, the American population of Greek descent is by a multiple larger than the American population of Turkish stock. In some of the biggest American states and municipalities, the constituency of Greek descent holds the political balance. Americans of Greek descent hold high political office. Americans of Greek descent are, in general, affluent. Some count among the most affluent men and women in the land. By a wide margin, Greek-Americans are more numerous and more influential in politics, science, business, and the arts than are Turkish-Americans.

Although Turkish-Americans are individually their Greek compatriots' equals in achievement, their collective impact upon American society is considerably less. It is unlikely that Turkish-Americans can ever break out of this ratio that is so unfavorable to them.

If any people is a history-conscious people, it is the Greek, and the Greek lobby in America has been highly successful in playing on the receptivity of the Americans of Greek descent to the appeal to history—a history written by passionately partial historians. In this history, Turkey is the chief villain. In the Greek version of history, Turkey has sought unrelentingly to dominate the Aegean Sea. The Greek lobby's effort has paid off to the manifest detriment of Turkey—and of American policy towards both Greece and Turkey.

At the time of this writing, both Greece and Turkey are the recipients of American assistance funds as proposed by the administration and as disbursed with the approval of Congress. The allocation of these funds, intended for the improvement of the recipients' military defense and national economy, is determined, so the administration has stated to Congress, by the recipients' respective contributions to the defense of the Atlantic Alliance of which both are members.

The administration deems the Turkish contribution to be larger than the Greek. It has done so by a number of criteria—the size of Turkish military forces assigned to the Alliance's common defense and Turkey's strategic location at the crossroads from the Black Sea to the Mediterranean and from Europe to the Middle East. By these criteria, so the American administration has argued, Turkey's contribution to common defense has been by a multiple larger than that of Greece.

Here I will not examine the validity of these criteria and of the administration's case. Suffice that the administration put its case before Congress, requesting its approval of a Turkish aid package larger than the Greek one. All Allies concurred—except Greece and the friends of Greece in the United States. Congress, rising to the challenge of the Greek lobby, rejected the administration's proposal for the Turkish aid package.

Although the administration never formally acquiesced to the ensuing compromise, Congress had its way. American aid to Greece would not be less than seven-tenths of the aid given to Turkey or, rather, Turkey would receive an assistance package no larger than ten-sevenths of the Greek one.

This "cap" on American aid to Turkey did not reflect the judgment of either NATO's military authorities or the U.S. Departments of State and Defense. It was the U.S. Congress or, rather, the Congressional committees that passed on the administration's request for the funding of the aid program—the power of the purse—that crafted the 7:10 formula and, overriding the anguished protest of the president, made it stick.[1]

Again, I will not here probe the rights and the wrongs of the Greek-Turkish imbroglio. Suffice that the Greek lobby made its case: it was the Turkish military threat to Greece, as alleged by the Greek lobby, and not the Soviet military threat to Europe, as perceived by the Alliance, that tilted U.S. policy to the side of Greece. Greece had not only stymied Turkey, it has also tweaked the nose of the Western superpower.

This episode, though it made the Turks very angry and stultified the Alliance, might be only a minor incident in the conduct of the United States' global policies. I have chosen it to illustrate the dilemma of American foreign policy. Can American democracy make foreign policy? Does the American president have the latitude to form and pursue foreign policies that he deems necessary on grounds of foreign policy and on these grounds alone? The Constitution says he can and must, for foreign policy *is* the policy of national security and, hence, has primacy over all conceivable national policies.

One of the greatest concerns of the American Founding Fathers was that the executive might be unable to carry out its proper functions, that it would be (in their term) "embarrassed," as it had been under the Articles of Confederation. To this end, they provided for a much stronger executive, particularly in the realm of war and peace. Indeed, several major contributions to *The Federalist Papers* were taken up with assuring Americans that the president would not be an elected monarch. Today, much of the president's power in foreign affairs has been taken away in the name of Congressional "oversight," but actually in the name of domestic politics, lobby politics.

When the administration yielded to the pressures of the Greek lobby and its congressional spokesmen, it clearly did not do so on grounds of national security. It was on the battlefield of domestic politics that the administration's case was lost. Greek-Americans are well represented in Congress, Turkish-Americans are not. Greek-Americans have tended to vote for the Democratic Party and to embrace causes that have not been dear to the Republican Party. This may not have been the crucial factor in the compromise on aid to Turkey. Human Rights lobbies, faulting Turkey for its alleged violations of human rights, have vocally opposed those of the administration's policies that might benefit Turkey.

The net result of this unseemly wrangle over American aid to one of America's staunchest allies, has been the defeat of the will of the president, choice of all the people, by the will of the Congressional majority in opposition, choice of all the people.

One hundred sixty years ago, Tocqueville gleaned a small dark cloud on the horizon of American democracy, the infringement on the orderly processes of democratic government by the *de facto* participation in the government of interest groups that, bypassing the processes of representative government as laid down by the Constitution, bring direct pressure to bear on the government. That, under the Constitution, they have no place in the government, does not diminish their power to bend the government to their will. In effect, American politics is the politics of the lobbies and the pressure groups they represent, operating in that grey area of "influence" left uncharted by the Constitution. Has it not always been so? Not being an expert on constitutional practice, my answer to this question is: probably, yes. Here, however, my concern is the bearing of this system—an unwritten system without rules—on the making of foreign policy.

For an indication of the consequences, ironically, one commentator has suggested we might look to France.

> During the Fourth Republic in France, a synonym for political chaos, the French regimented themselves into a myriad of small factions made up of people who agreed with one another absolutely and permitted no departure whatsoever from orthodoxy. Post-Vietnam America is in the process of achieving similar results, through the proliferation of pressure groups that are indistinguishable from radical political parties in all respects except their preference for operating behind the scenes through the mechanism of the two great traditional parties.[2]

Notes

1. "A 1978 amendment to the Foreign Assistance Act of 1961 (Pub.L. 95–384) stipulated that aid to Turkey and Greece should 'be designed to insure that the present balance of military strength among countries in the region...is preserved.' The Greek government determined that balance would be met when Greece received 70 percent of whatever amount of military aid was approved for Turkey. A majority of Congress, led by members with substantial Greek-American constituencies, agreed with Athens. Consequently, the 7:10 ratio has been the de facto definition of the Aegean military balance since 1979. The executive branch persistently resisted this formula, arguing that Turkey's strategic importance far exceeds Greece's, and that much of the Greek allotment should go to Turkey. Nonetheless, the 7:10 ratio has been maintained rigidly by Congress." Duncan L. Clarke and Daniel O'Connor, "U.S. Base-Rights Payments after the Cold War," *Orbis*, Summer 1993, citing Monteagle Stearns, *Entangled Allies: U.S. Policy toward Greece, Turkey, and Cyprus* (New York: Council on Foreign Relations, 1992), p. 451.
2. Alexander M. Haig, Jr., with Charles McGarry, *Inner Circles: How America Changed the World. A Memoir* (New York: Warner Books, 1992), p. 562.

13

Idealism versus Realism

This book is not about the politics of American democracy. It is about the politics of American foreign policy—about the impact of American domestic politics upon American diplomacy. Alexis de Tocqueville, placing America in the "front rank of nations," tells us laconically how America has attained her place among nations: the "principal instrument" of American power is freedom, and its servant, commerce. "The conquests of the American are...gained by the plough share," he wrote, and by that, of course, he meant by economic effort. At the time of Tocqueville's brilliant observation, this was true—as true as any statement about the American ethos could have been. It is still true today: Americans abhor military conquest; they seek, now as they did then, to accomplish their ends by "relying upon personal interest," and giving free scope to the innate strength and common sense—the prudence—of the people. American foreign policy makers, too, have not been able to jump across their shadow; freedom remains the "principal instrument" of American diplomacy.[1]

A graph drawn of the fluctuations of American foreign policy decisions would illustrate the continuity of the reliance on the force of the economic, rather than the military, argument. Even at the occasion of the grimmest confrontations in American history, American foreign policy has had, by a conditioned reflex, recourse to economic means, such as economic sanctions and suspension of Most Favored Nations Status agreements. That conflict between nations can be resolved by the use of economic power rather than by military means is one of the most deeply and widely held convictions of the American people—as is the conviction that no one is more firmly dedicated to peace than they. To doubt the validity of these assumptions is to doubt the popular conception of foreign policy—of what it ought to be in order to serve the best interests of the American people.

Yet, there is still history with its contradictions, without which existence on this globe would be as meaningless as life without love and hate. The most pacific among the great nations has fought the most destructive wars in history, and, at one time or another, occupied vast territories not its own.

Two schools of thought, theoretically, contest for the formation of American foreign policy: idealism and realism. The idealist school of thought stands for the worldwide affirmation of American values, all of which can be subsumed under the idea of freedom with justice for all peoples. The foreign policy of democracy is democracy.

Not that the idealists are unmindful of the national interest and the exigencies of power politics. Quite to the contrary: they hold that domestic welfare needs to underpin the projection of U.S. power, military and economic, into world politics, and that America, in order to keep her place in the world must, first and foremost, eradicate socioeconomic inequities at home.

Quintessentially, idealist American foreign policy is Wilsonian foreign policy: war, if fought, shall be fought in order to end all wars "by making the world safe for democracy." National security shall be guaranteed by collective security; a League of Nations shall put an end to the anarchy of power politics and usher in a new world order. Now, of course, it is the United Nations that will and must succeed where the League has failed.

Realists demur. Between the two World Wars, they point out, the United States vested its prestige in a major initiative of multilateral diplomacy: the Kellogg-Briand Pact.[2] But since the signatories of the Pact did not care to match the military deployment of the aggressors—Germany, Italy, and Japan—its impact on world affairs was nil.

Likewise, although the United Nations has had its uses, it still cannot address the great issues of war and peace more convincingly than its predecessor. In Iraq, the United Nations, at the pressing behest of American diplomacy, presented a united diplomatic front. But the unilateral price paid by U.S. diplomacy for U.N. condemnation of aggression was massive. The bulk of the firepower was American.

Realists argue that the correlations of domestic welfare with national security; of a free market economy with democracy; of democracy with a nation's peaceful disposition in international politics, has not, historically, been as high as current wisdom says. A prosperous economy and a bountiful system of socioeconomic welfare do not translate, by themselves, into national security, not to speak of effective defense against a surprise attack by a leaner, tougher, and better-armed aggressor.

Paradoxically, then, it is the realist who rejects the primacy of economics in social relations as a sure guide to international relations. For the determinants of a state's behavior in international politics, realists place greater weight than do idealists on non-material factors, such as patriotism and nationalism.

For example, Russia now seems amenable to far-reaching political and economic reforms that might culminate in the establishment of a more democratic government and a freer economy. If this comes to pass, will the Russian people, purged of communist idolatry, be less patriotic, less nationalist, and less possessive about the imperial realm than they were, let us say, under Czar Nicholas II? Realists point out that geography and national character are not as changeable as are political systems and ideologies. The Russian people have remained true to their historical sense of mission at immense sacrifice, under czarist as well as communist rule. If the fall of communism has not diminished their legendary patriotism, realists warn, the problems of U.S. policy towards the new Russia will be much the same as they were before the collapse of the Soviet Union.

Above, I have sought to encapsulate the essence of American thought about world politics as idealist and realist respectively. All generalizations risk oversimplification and so do these. In fact, there is no clear line of demarcation between the two camps. The realists have popular pragmatism on their side; the idealists draw for support on the popular reservoir of good will towards all of mankind that spills over the harsh limits of national self-interest.

Yet, most Americans, passing judgement on the foreign policies administered by the executive, seem to be ambivalent. Thus, for example, most Americans were ready to wage total war against Iraq; but most Americans were equally ready to sanction humanitarian assistance to the Iraqi people, breaching the wall of economic sanctions that were to have enforced Iraq's compliance with the Allies cease-fire conditions— an inconsistency of which Saddam Hussein did not fail to take advantage.

Most Americans condemned the Octogenarians' lethal repression of democratic stirrings in China. But most Americans would rather do business with China than impose punitive sanctions on the Octogenarians and would rather leave it to the workings of international economics to acculturate communist China to the liberal world order.

Most Americans are eager to cash in on the "peace dividends" accruing from the collapse of the Soviet empire. But they are willing to fund an arms budget that, but for marginal deductions, still leaves American deterrence power intact.

Referenda and Polls

This tug-of-war between foreign policy and its costs, and domestic welfare and costs, is likely to remain undecided as long as American foreign policy is made by short-term office holders, and by successive popular referenda—the public opinion polls. That these spontaneous, unstructured expressions of the popular will are not called by their right name and are highly volatile does not make them less effective. The foreign-policy decision maker needs to "think himself" into the popular mind. It is no longer he who teaches the people the realities of foreign policy, as Edmund Burke said he should. Rather, it is he who is being instructed by the people, issue by issue, about what his decision ought to be.

In this way, the making of American foreign policy has become a high-risk business. The stakes—national security—are higher than they have ever been. But so, too, are the political risks to the presidency— *fons et origo* of American foreign policy. At each move on the checker board of international politics, the president risks his office and his party's chances of fielding his successor. If any kind of national policy making is now apt to turn into an issue of participatory politics, it is the making of foreign policy. In Congress, American foreign policy is now being ground out in several major and several minor Congressional committees, most of which were set up to deal with matters other than foreign affairs.

In this book, I have argued for a foreign policy that, first and foremost, defends and advances the cause of democratization; but I oppose with equal vigor the "democratization" of foreign policy, an inherently elite undertaking.

The referendum is the most direct and most spontaneous expression of democratization. It is also the simplest. The U.S. Constitution (unlike the French Constitution[3]) is moot on the subject of referenda in the formation of American foreign policy, and, so far as I know, national referenda have not been called in America. But they have been proposed. For example, the idea of introducing the referendum into U.S. foreign policy was put forward by Alan Toleson, in a *New York Times* op-ed article. Tonelson argued that, with the end of the cold war,

> great possibilities are...emerging for further democratizing foreign policy—and specifically for enabling Americans directly to authorize or veto policies already under way or in the works. An ideal place to begin would be a national referendum on U.S. aid to El Salvador.[4]

Even without formal referenda, however, the continuous use of polls means that American foreign policies are increasingly shaped by soundings of the public mood, continuous and recorded by state-of-the-art devices of measurement. Thus, the maker of foreign policy has, whenever he so chooses, highly accurate indicators of the swings of public opinion on foreign policy in the making.

All too frequently, foreign policy is shaped by these public opinion polls that measure, ad hoc, the popular support a foreign policy maker can—or cannot—expect for his creation. The process is unstructured; it is untidy; it functions by improvisation; it has not been institutionalized; and there is no name for it. But everyone knows that it supplements the proceedings of Congress, which was supposed to articulate the will of the people but no longer does so. Today, the voice of the people speaks with a plebiscitary stutter.

One of the problems with this process of foreign policy by referendum, or opinion poll, which amounts to the same thing, was clearly stated by Jean-François Revel:

> The frustration is that public moods about foreign affairs so often reflect internal, domestic trends. They oscillate according to inner psychological needs, rather than to factual changes in international life.... You cannot have a view of domestic and economic affairs totally disconnected from the facts. It may suit your peace of mind to deny that there is inflation or labor unrest, but that illusion won't survive the next bill you have to pay or the next strike of the sanitation workers. In foreign affairs, on the contrary, you may live for years with an illusion before an indisputable test clearly demonstrates its fallibility. You are able to deny or underestimate or forget a military threat until the day it materializes.[5]

Yet, even Revel does not fully capture how "disconnected from the facts" public opinion may be on foreign affairs. In June 1988, after President Ronald Reagan had spent virtually his entire presidency trying to enlist support for the contras against Nicaragua's Sandinista government, polls of American public opinion produced the following results: 7 percent thought the contras and the Sandinistas were fighting in Southeast Asia; 48 percent could not name Nicaragua as the country where the conflict was taking place; and 61 percent thought Moscow was backing a communist insurgency against the Sandinistas.[6] At the same time, to use Tonelson's example of El Salvador, 43 percent thought that country was unfriendly to the United States; 35 percent thought it had a pro-Soviet communist government; and only 4 percent knew it faced a communist insurgency.[7]

Notes

1. Alexis de Tocqueville, *Democracy in America,* vol. 1, ed. Phillips Bradley (New York, Vintage Books, 1945), p. 452.
2. The Kellogg-Briand Pact (also called the Pact of Paris) was a multilateral agreement attempting to eliminate war as an instrument of national policy. It was signed on August 27, 1928.
3. Article 2 of the French Constitution says: "National sovereignty belongs to the people, which shall exercise this sovereignty through its representatives and through the referendum."
4. Alan Toleson, "Foreign Policy by Referendum," *The New York Times,* April 16, 1990.
5. Jean-François Revel, "Reflections on Foreign Policy and Public Opinion," *Public Opinion,* July/August, 1978, pp. 15–16.
6. *The Wall Street Journal,* June 6, 1988.
7. *The Philadelphia Inquirer,* June 3, 1988.

14

The American Diplomatic Establishment

The American people's indifference, if not aversion, to the history of international politics has been at the root of Americans' mounting confusion about their foreign policy.

What matters most in policy making is the maker's clear understanding of his position at any given time. Where he will end up and where he started from are data he can approach only asymptotically, since there is no end to history—and no beginning.

The result is a tendency to act in the present. Lightening diplomatic reversals raise yesterday's unspeakable transgressor to dignified partnership in the search for peace. What, yesterday, no one thought of is today acclaimed as the achievement of seasoned statecraft. Yesterday's ally is told today that he would be well advised to fend for himself and think of yesterday's common enemy as a future partner in the quest for peace. The word for this unseemly behavior—diplomacy by improvisation—is pragmatism: the lack of principle as a way of life.

Prince Metternich is supposed to have said that in foreign affairs only improvisation endures. He is also quoted having said that his mission as Imperial Austria's chancellor and foreign minister had been to "prop up rotten institutions." Since he spectacularly failed in his endeavor, statesmanship, especially American statesmanship, has nothing to learn from this sleek confidence man.

Up until the rise of the United States as the predominant Western power, all chancelleries considered it axiomatic that foreign policy should *not* be made on the marketplace. Populism in America has demonstrated that, in fact, this is the place it must be made. A constitutionally chosen government can be brought to its knees by direct action—by mass demonstrations, media campaigns, publicized confrontations with the agencies of public order, and the covert action of lobbies committed to "influencing" the government. In many "Hours of Truth," the makers of U.S. foreign policy, rather than standing fast on their constitutional mandate, have retreated before populist pressures.

That is how, year after year, the U.S. government loses its case for the rational allocation of American military and economic assistance to Greece and Turkey. That is how, on a vaster scale, it lost its case for enforcing the settlement of the Vietnam War. That war might have been the wrong war in the wrong place. But it was lost in a quite different place—the streets of America—and populist action made its point.

The Constitution vests the president with the "power, by and with the advice of Senate, to make Treaties, to appoint Ambassadors, and to receive Ambassadors." The Constitution leaves it to the Congress to provide the president with the instruments he needs to make foreign policy, to wit, to "regulate commerce with foreign nations," and, when he so chooses, with the appropriate military force to insure "common defense." It is within the power of Congress to "declare war" and, thus, to continue foreign policy by Carl von Clausewitz's "other means."

These passages, culled from the Constitution, summarize the Founders' provisions for making foreign policy—and paying for it. They are both scant and stringent. They differ considerably from the provisions regulating foreign-policy making in the constitutions of most other democratic states.

What the Constitution does *not* say about foreign policy—its formulation and conduct—that has been as consequential for the international relationships of the United States as has been what it says explicitly. The power it vests in the president, though sweeping, is contingent on restrictions, as sweeping, that can annul it. It is this contradiction—a magnificent contradiction—that has baffled the United States's fellow players on the field of international politics. Is not all that foreign statesmen need to do in the way of clarification to read more carefully the U.S. Constitution? This is sage advice.

It would be more helpful still had not, at some memorable occasions, American presidents, pledged to the defense of the Constitution, miscalculated massively the latitude that the Constitution gives the American president in his capacity as the exclusive maker of foreign policy. When, in 1919, President Wilson, at the height of his popularity at home and abroad, urged all the peoples to join in a League of Nations, he did not anticipate that, in 1921, the U.S. Senate would block the United States's entry into the League, the transcendent objective of his diplomacy. The long and unhappy story of U.S. attempts at negotiations with Khomeini's Iran would be incomprehensible without due allowance being made for the root cause of this diplomatic disaster: the adversary relationship between two branches of the U.S. government—or, rather, the failure of the executive to reckon with it.

America's Diplomatic Style

Johann Wolfgang von Goethe's long life spanned the dynastic wars of the eighteenth century, the Napoleonic Wars, and the rise of republican government throughout the Americas.[1] Concerning the last of these, he failed to leave posterity a comprehensive analysis, but, drawing from his readings and from American visitors to Weimar, his boundless curiosity and uncanny prescience had focused on the United States, a country so unlike the old states of Europe. He told one of his callers that Americans were fortunate "to have no ruins"—to have no long and tragic history to forget.

The past, a thousand years of feudalism and dynastic wars, did not weigh down on the new Republic. The Americans, unimpressed by the glitter of the European courts, whose costs had been extorted for generations from a voiceless populace, brought to international diplomacy the spirit as well as the style of an egalitarian society. Two hundred years ago, the somber dress of the American envoys to the European states—plain frock coats versus the beribboned, brocaded adornments of courtly society—signified more than the frugality of a strapped and struggling state. American democracy had no place for privilege, be it only sartorial.

The diplomatic establishment of the United States has grown vastly. The scribes that assisted the first secretary of state in drafting his messages to his ministers abroad have multiplied by the thousands. In 1850, 218 persons serviced the Department of State. In 1992, 10,108 officials cared for the foreign policies of the United States.

In American diplomacy, as in other undertakings, sheer quantity does not necessarily turn into quality. The present generation of American diplomats might well be superior to their predecessors in some, though not in all, skills of the profession. Still, little has changed in the spirit that drives American diplomacy. Even its forms have changed little.

But the world has changed. Though distinctly American, the style of American diplomacy, like that of most things American, has lent itself to easy and eager adaptation by other peoples, including some most hostile to the United States. De Tocqueville's famous observation that democracies are unable to act with secrecy and dispatch in foreign policy is deeply rooted in American experience, and professional secrecy and dispatch, after all, are the favorite tools, along with expediency, that distinguish the ancien regime of international diplomacy. In its rise to world power, the United States brought to diplomacy not only its ever increasing geopolitical power but also its view of the world.

Having been in the diplomatic business for centuries, the Chancelleries of Europe professed, not so many years ago, to look down with amused contempt on the quaint ways of American diplomacy. American diplomacy was apt to cut across protocol, hence it was derided as uncouth. American diplomacy tended to be blunt; hence it was derided as simplistic. Since then, the prestige of American diplomacy has risen commensurately with its immense achievements.

The American Image

Yet, the American way in diplomacy does not appear to foreign publics as straight and as open as Americans like to see it. To clear up this discrepancy and the resultant misunderstandings, this task could be safely left to the agencies of public relations—were the American people not at odds with themselves about the goals and the conduct of their foreign policy.

I have pointed out above the American people's historical aversion towards foreign commitments, notably in the shape of men and money. In this sense, the average American is isolationist. Told that he cannot opt out of world politics for the sake of his security and prosperity, he would do exactly that, were it not for his belief in the sagacity of his chosen leaders. This layer of trust has been strong enough to support the momentous decisions that took American power to every corner of the globe and to the top of world politics. It has been rent in Vietnam; it held in Iraq. American foreign policy narrows down to the question as to whether that layer of trust will survive the next test intact.

But America speaks an idiom of its own creation. It leads the world in semantic study and in the courage of bold metaphors and strident slogans. It is also the unquiet land of semantic confusion.

To be isolated is a condition and, generally, an involuntary one, and, hence, an undesirable one. Americans have never conceived of themselves as being isolated from the world in that sense. It has never signified a withdrawal from the world. It has always been selective—and, hence, has appeared to foreign observers as inconsistent and enigmatic.

American diplomacy has striven mightily to put right the misunderstandings that, on some critical occasions, have upset America's friends and allies and, worse, sent the wrong signals to America's enemies. (Witness Secretary of State Dean Acheson's statement omitting South Korea from the array of the United States's strategic priorities![2])

Even so, non-Americans have wondered if American isolationism is a doctrine of poised disinterest in international politics, or the mask of a new kind of expansionism. Shocking as might be the thought to Americans that their immense contribution to international peace and prosperity could be mistaken for giant steps on the path of imperialism, it does not seem implausible to countless millions, if not the majority of mankind.

It happens to be a silly thought—as massively silly as the silliness of Marxist-Leninist ideas on imperialism that molder in the attic of communist ideology. Silly or not, it saddles American diplomacy with the crucially important task of rectification. The problem might be one of communication and, therefore, soluble by the methods of an art of which the United States is the master. For a certainty, it will not go away during this and the next generation.

American Universalism

This and other "misunderstandings" that have tarnished the fair image of American democracy in world affairs would be more tractable, were it not for Washington's propensity to couch diplomatic initiatives in universalist language and identify the American national interests with the best interests of all mankind—its propensity to claim to speak for the universe rather than for one nation among nations. President Wilson's appeal to the world—to "make the world safe for democracy"—was inspired by a noble vision; his redemptory rhetoric raised the hackles of the foreign and American politicians whose support he needed most to win the peace, this being not the least cause of his failure.

America's universalist appeal has the support of history. The foreign policy of a multi-ethnic state cannot help setting supranational goals or, rather, squaring national goals with the memories and aspirations of its ethnic components. In this endeavor, America has succeeded brilliantly. To the discomfiture of America's enemies, divided loyalties did not hamper American intervention in World War II. Since then, the national consensus has been sealed by common achievement at home and abroad, and, above all, by that great homogenizer, the American school. Multiethnic America has come of age.

(In the wake of Pearl Harbor, populist xenophobia sent the Nisei population of the Pacific coast and Hawaii to concentration camps. Most of the male, adult victims of this brutal administrative blunder, upon their release from captivity, rallied to the flag and served with distinction in the U.S. Army. If any ethnic component of the American Union has shown that the national consensus holds, it is the Americans of Japanese descent.)

American diplomacy is the diplomacy of a multi-ethnic democracy that is increasingly populist and uncompromisingly egalitarian. It has struck out on new paths. Like all successful innovators, America-in-world-affairs remembers from the past what it chooses to remember and forgets what it chooses to forget. There is in the catechism of American diplomacy no place for notions reminiscent of the cabinet diplomacy, the *Grosse Politik* of the Great Powers of old, made in secrecy by an elite of decision makers who vaunt themselves to be the sole possessor of the arcanum of diplomacy. American diplomacy has spurned these snobbish pretensions. What it cannot snub, however, is the populist demand that American foreign policy reflect democratic values even as its respects the realism of power politics.

To square this circle is the burden of American statesmanship. On the face of it, the American people expect their foreign policy makers to do the impossible—serve the cause of both international justice and the national self-interest beyond the law. It is part of America's mythological heritage that the impossible can be done if one tries hard enough. In the last forty-five years—from the Longest Day to the Victory of Containment—American statesmanship tried hard enough and squared the circle.

Notes

1. Johann Wolfgang von Goethe was born in 1749 and died in 1832.

2. On January 12, 1950, Secretary of State Dean Acheson made a speech to the National Press Club that discussed the "defensive perimeter" of the United States. The speech made no direct reference to South Korea as lying within that defensive perimeter, although the defensive perimeter was said to include the Aleutian Islands, Japan, Okinawa, and the Philippines. Acheson's words were: "This defensive perimeter runs along the Aleutians to Japan and then goes to the Ryukyus. We hold important defense positions in the Ryukyu Islands and these we will continue to hold.... The defensive perimeter runs from the Ryukyus to the Philippine Islands." See Dean Acheson, *Present at the Creation* (New York: W.W. Norton and Company, 1969), p. 357.

    North Korea invaded South Korea on June 25, 1950.

    Acheson later claimed that he had not referred to South Korea because he had consulted a March 1949 speech on the subject by General Douglas MacArthur, and that speech had made the same omission. In any event, the speech "is known chiefly for the famous passage in which Acheson failed to include South Korea within the American defense perimeter in the Far East." See David S. McLellan, *Dean Acheson: The State Department Years* (New York: Dodd, Mead, and Company, 1976), p. 209.

15

American Attitudes towards Diplomacy

Up to World War I and, in some important respects, until World War II, the American people did not view diplomacy as the first line of national defense. Since they did not think that they needed any defense against any and all of the Great Powers, they were content with an army capable of defending their continental borders and with a navy capable of guarding all the Americas against foreign, that is, European, intervention. Happily, these objectives being strictly limited geographically and the strategic asset of remoteness from the likely flashpoints being cost free, national defense claimed but a negligible slice of the tax dollar.

Americans did not think of themselves as actors on the stage of power politics. Generations of emigrants from Europe had sought and found in America a haven from compulsory military service. They had voted against European militarism by buying passage on an Atlantic steamer. They and their descendents would never vote themselves back into the hateful system that they praised themselves fortunate to have escaped. Americans have never been and never will be militarists.

Paradoxically, however, Americans take pride in their martial prowess. Americans have chosen from the ranks of their military some of their greatest leaders. Again, paradoxically, Americans like uniforms and the glitter of military insignia. They rejoice in acclaiming the victorious military hero. Since the civilian control of the military has been the most durable and least controversial of all American political institutions, Americans feel free to celebrate the military virtues. They know they will not surrender their liberties to the "man on horseback"—or is it now the man on a computer-programmed tank?

In nineteenth-century Europe, the military as a class ranked at the top of the social heap. In their public appearances, the monarchs wore military uniforms. At ceremonial occasions, the diplomatic representatives of all European states, with the exception of the Helvetian Republic, wore uniforms (with and without swords). Diplomatic officials were interrelated, socially and bureaucratically, with military officers. A Europe-wide net of family relations joined both establishments. Members of the same family served both—one or several sons as military officers, one or several sons as diplomats. Both careers were closed by tacit agreement and, in some countries, explicitly, to members of other social classes.

Some breakthroughs occurred. Outsiders "made it"—mostly by virtue of great wealth rather than exceptional military-diplomatic competence. Not so long ago, diplomats were assumed to possess "independent" means—private wealth. The government's financial contribution was paltry or nil. The rewards were social prestige and dignified fun.

This European diplomatic tradition is a hardy plant. In most countries, it has withstood the blight of war and revolution. High-ranking Soviet diplomats wore gold braided uniforms—as did most other high-ranking servants of the communist state under the writ of the dictatorship of the proletariat. British diplomats—be they the agents of a Labour government, be they at the orders of a Conservative government—still wear the court dress, complete with gold braid, feathery head gear and sword, *de rigueur* one hundred years ago. Not a few Third World countries have adopted these garments of sartorial protocol.

Although the First World War swept the territorial aristocracies of Europe from the high places of government, hereditary aristocracy has stayed on, with remarkable tenacity, in one sector of the European job market, a minute one, yet one of crucial importance to the state: in the manning of foreign offices and diplomatic missions abroad, aristocrats still supply a quota of the requisite talent that is disproportionately larger than their share in government employment as a whole. One reason for this skewed proportion has been the cosmopolitan and multilingual tradition of the European aristocracies. The other is the sheer inertia of Europe's social structure that has withstood the forces of change that, on the face of it, shook its very foundations, and yet, in fact, left it intact.

From the beginning, the American people have been of two minds about diplomacy: On the one hand, they felt that America needed proficient diplomats to cope with the wiles of European diplomacy; on the other, even their own diplomats stood in the odor of being smooth and slick intriguers, rather than forthright and simple men such as Americans thought themselves to be. Benjamin Franklin personified the American's ideal representative: embodying homespun virtue and simple deportment, yet canny in doing the Republic's business.

Much of this popular aversion to the diplomatic profession and its indelibly foreign ways—secret covenants, secretly arrived at; and the braided protocol of Westphalian vintage—has spilled over from the age of political innocence into the age of American world power. Americans would still happily trade world power and its haunting risks for the simple joys of staying home, so long as home means a vast continent. America, sufficient under itself, would happily off-load a long list of its superpower tools. And the American diplomatic establishment, having never excelled in gaining popular affection, would be one of the first—possibly *the* first—of the branches of government to fall under the axe of sequester.

But here again we face another paradox. Though no people are as eager to embrace the world as is the American—the slogans of "One World" are of American coinage and dissemination—their gut response to the challenges of that One World is today as isolationist as it has ever been. Americans might wish to embrace the world; but they are deeply skeptical about its politics and, all things being equal, are determined to keep out of it.

That bears thought. Though an enormous effort has gone into polishing the image of American diplomacy and popularizing American foreign policy, all things being equal, most Americans would dispense with international politics and its professional personnel, the diplomats. If the American public has generally been reluctant to buy the product of this public-relations effort and, in some memorable instances, has declined the offer altogether, the failure should be ascribed to causes that lie much deeper than public-relations blunders, as frequent and grievous as those might have been. Americans perceive of foreign-policy making as an elitist pursuit—and in that they have been quite right.

In Europe, the foreign policy establishments have always been buttressed by a long tradition of exclusivity and trust. The conduct of foreign affairs, people thought, was best left to a small corps of professionals, well connected with the upper levels of government and at ease in the upper strata of the "Good Society" to which, but for some exceptions that confirmed the rule, they belonged by birth.

In Europe, democratic government is parliamentary government. Prime ministers are the chiefs of the parliamentary majority, be it one party or composed of several parties, thus forming a coalition. When the chief of government and the Cabinet of Ministers decide upon a major initiative in foreign policy, they need not travel any distance in order to gain its approval by the elected representatives of the people. The political party or parties composing the government dominates the legislature. The opposition has its say, of course, and the commotion can be piercingly audible. But once the opposition has spoken, majoritarian will, articulated in Parliament, carries the day—and the government proceeds to do what it told Parliament it meant to do. The idea that a government can be divided between an executive duly elected by majority vote and an opposition also duly elected by majority vote is as puzzling to Europeans as is to Americans the ability of parliamentary government to function without the input, solicited or unsolicited, of the legislative committees, not to speak of committees controlled by the opposition.

How does the informal system of interest groups and lobbies interact with these two forms of democracy? In Europe, organized pressure groups—as, for example, the agricultural lobbies, bringing their powerful influence to bear on national governments and the government of the European community—supply services to their sponsors that differ not a wit from those mandated and paid for by the corresponding interests converging on Washington. Yet, great as is their influence, it is not as pervasive as is the lobby culture in Washington.

The reason lies with the nature of parliamentary government. The concentration of lobby pressure on one target, the administration—creature of the parliamentary majority—suffices to produce the desired results. Washington lobbies operate on two fronts—the administration and Congress. Even when the same party controls both the White House and the Capitol—as (before the Clinton administration) had not been the case during the last twenty years except for one presidential term[1]—the system still proves exasperatingly cumbersome and time consuming.

When the control is divided—as it has been but for the said exception—it denies the foreign-policy maker what he needs most: swiftness of decision. The lobbyist is endowed with a precious advantage: room for maneuver between the executive and Congress. If the desired result cannot be obtained by persuading the administration, then members of Congress may be more susceptible to the arguments of the lobbyist.

In addition, divided government deprives the foreign-policy maker of a second critical factor: protection against premature disclosure of contemplated policies. If lobbyists possess any one skill, it is the management of public relations—to gain publicity favorable to the "interest" that employs them, and to disseminate material unfavorable to the cause that stands in the "interest's" way. With divided government giving the lobbyist a partisan motive on which to work, the inner secrets of government can be pried loose for his interest's purposes with far greater ease, in the name of the public's right to know.

In Europe, too, the public has the "right to know." But the question—as agonizing to the foreign-policy maker in Europe as to his American counterpart—is: when must the public be told? No less important, when has the time come for disclosing a foreign policy not only to the American public but, consequently, also to the country that is a party—the other party—to the diplomatic dialogue? Having had to seek an answer to this question in real life situations, I believe that, in a parliamentary democracy, the foreign-policy maker is better protected than is the American, trying to balance the public's right to know with exigencies of diplomacy, a diplomacy that deals with concrete issues concretely, rather than "public" diplomacy for partisan show. Some of the most crucial foreign policies have been written or talked to death long before they could have been tested by events.

Notes

1. As the following table of the last twenty-plus years shows, the White House and Congress have rarely been held by the same party:
   - 1969-1971: White House (R); Senate (D); House (D)
   - 1971-1973: White House (R); Senate (D); House (D)
   - 1973-1975: White House (R); Senate (D); House (D)
   - 1975-1977: White House (R); Senate (D); House (D)
   - 1977-1979: White House (D); Senate (D); House (D)
   - 1979-1981: White House (D); Senate (D); House (D)
   - 1981-1983: White House (R); Senate (R); House (D)
   - 1983-1985: White House (R); Senate (R); House (D)
   - 1985-1987: White House (R); Senate (R); House (D)
   - 1987-1989: White House (R); Senate (D); House (D)
   - 1989-1991: White House (R); Senate (D); House (D)
   - 1991-1993: White House (R); Senate (D); House (D)
   - 1993-1995: White House (D); Senate (D); House (D)

16

The Military-Industrial Complex

If any man could claim to have been the founder of the Atlantic Alliance, it was President Truman, cunning politician, subtle statesman, and homespun populist. If proof is needed for the workings of divine predestination in the affairs of nations, this most unlikely maker of global history supplied it. The American people followed him unto ground they had vowed never to tread: a long-term commitment to international power politics.

But if Truman's populist touch launched the fateful enterprise, it was his successor's immense popularity and professional expertise that ensured the conversion of America's massive military intervention in Europe into coalition diplomacy. President Eisenhower asked for and received America's unstinting contribution in men and money to the making of the most powerful peacetime alliance in history. This contribution was as huge as it was unprecedented. And it was manifestly popular.

To the pained surprise of the military and industrial constituencies of the Atlantic Alliance, President Eisenhower, on the eve of his retirement from office, saw fit to warn his countrymen against a peril to the nation that it did not have to face under his predecessors. In his farewell address, delivered on January 17, 1961, he spoke as follows:

> Until the latest of our world conflicts, the United States had no armaments industry. American makers of plowshares could, with time and as required, make swords as well. But now we can no longer risk emergency improvisation of national defense; we have been compelled to create a permanent armaments industry of vast proportions. Added to this, 3½ million men and women are directly engaged in the Defense Establishment. We annually spend on military security more than the net income of all United States corporations.

> This conjunction of an immense Military Establishment and a large arms industry is new in the American experience. The total influence—economic, political, even

spiritual—is felt in every city, every statehouse, every office of the Federal Government. We recognize the imperative need for this development. Yet we must not fail to comprehend its grave implications. Our toil, resources, and livelihood are all involved; so is the very structure of our society.

In the councils of government we must guard against the acquisition of unwarranted influence whether sought or unsought, by the military-industrial complex. The potential for the disastrous rise of misplaced power exists and will persist.

We must never let the weight of this combination endanger our liberties or democratic processes. We should take nothing for granted. Only an alert and knowledgeable citizenry can compel the proper meshing of the huge industrial and military machinery of defense with our peaceful methods and goals so that security and liberty may prosper together.[1]

The president's address stated a dilemma that is as old as democracy: how to reconcile the exigencies of national defense with the claims of the domestic economy—how to reconcile democracy's disposition to the pacific pursuit of prosperity with the martial virtues that inspire fighting men and count trade for less than the production of arms.

It is as if the ghost of Tocqueville had hovered over the president at work on his political testament. More than a century before the president's disquisition on peace and war, and long before America joined the ranks of the Great Powers, Tocqueville wrote:

No protracted war can fail to endanger the freedom of a democratic country. Not indeed that, after every victory, is it to be apprehended that the victorious generals will possess themselves by force of the supreme power, after the manner of Sylla and Caesar: the danger is of another kind. War does not always give over democratic communities to military government, but it must invariably and immeasurably increase the powers of civil government; it must almost compulsorily concentrate the direction of all men and the management of all things in the hands of the administration. If it lead not to despotism by sudden violence, it prepares men for it more gently by their habits. All those who seek to destroy the liberties of a democratic nation ought to know that war is the surest and the shortest means to accomplish it. This is the first axiom of the science.[2]

The president's voice, though less sonorous than Tocqueville's prose, carried a similar message not only to all the places where decisions on war and peace were being made but also to all places where public opinion was made. His message took the world by surprise; it shook the "complex," in part because, though tightly argued, it lent itself—like all great political statements—to gross misinterpretations, such as the film *Dr. Strangelove.* It lent itself the more easily to such misrepresentations because the president refrained from spelling out who manned the ramparts of the "complex." For most Americans, it sufficed that their premier soldier held these concerns. In any event, his message was resoundingly popular. No one—certainly not the putative members of the complex—cared to disagree publicly with the president.

The making and selling of arms has been a singularly unpopular occupation in all democratic lands, and the odium of the vocation has rubbed off on the civilian and military bureaucracies that administer the arms budget. Thus, there is nothing mysterious about the impact of the president's speech on public opinion: it was stunningly popular; it expressed the historic aversion of American democracy towards the compulsion and the hierarchy of a standing military establishment in the midst of a permissive and egalitarian society. President Eisenhower, during his long career as a professional soldier, could not have helped noting the popular tendencies that, as Tocqueville put it, are "produced by the equality of condition... [and] concur to quench the military spirit."[3] Some of the most popular leaders of American democracy were soldiers—victorious ones. Yet the personal popularity of these men did not extend to their profession.

Yet, if war is merely the continuation of foreign policy by other means, as Clausewitz taught us, then it is the foreign-policy maker—ultimately the chief executive—who bears responsibility for the use of the production and employment of lethal "other means."[4] Each foreign policy has a military price tag from negligible to horrendous, from no arms at all to exorbitantly costly "weapons of mass destruction." In selecting his policy, the executive necessarily chooses the manufacture and sale of arms that goes with it. So, too, it is he who must determine when diplomacy alone no longer suffices to insure the national interest and when the military needs to be called upon to secure it, and his decision will be contingent on the military capabilities that he has at his disposal.

America's investment in arms in the postwar years was unprecedented for peacetime, second only to its investment in social welfare, and undoubtedly that investment is laced by waste and corruption—as is social welfare and virtually every major public undertaking in the country. In the case of arms, this propensity is further aggravated by the unique economic structure of the arms trade: the federal government is the one and only customer of countless private contractors. The interdependence of contractors and subcontractors, and of sub-subcontractors, is bewilderingly complex. It has spawned a hybrid system in which private business interlocks with government.

This worried Eisenhower, as it did Tocqueville. If, as Tocqueville held, the democratic state tends towards centralization and, hence, the extension of its writ to the free and uncontrolled margins of civility, than the vicissitudes of the "military-industrial complex" afford a preview of how this "weakness" of democracy might stand democracy on its head. That this feat might be achieved with the help of impeccably democratic procedures, does not make it less offensive to the spirit of liberty.

All of this is true. But if President Eisenhower had excised from his address the celebrated phrase, he could still have made his point, a point that no one could have made more authoritatively than he. The munitions industry—encouraged by the pressing demands for its goods and services—had tended to take for granted its place in the national budget. The voices of its spokesmen had grown too strident. Budgetary controls were too loose. Not all the profits of the trade reflected reasonable costs. No doubt the "complex" sheltered some oddballs and malodorous profiteers of the public bounty—as does any national enterprise involving huge outlays authorized under the pressure of great and unpredictable events.

America had conclusively fought a World War and, though not quite as conclusively, several limited ones. Now the American people ardently wished to turn from the exertions of war to the pursuit of happiness at home. In his speech, President Eisenhower, unfailingly sensitive to the nation's mood, marked the turn. His message was powerful.

But he chose to speak in the tradition of populist oratory, not telling his nationwide audience exactly who were the members of the complex nor how the complex exerted its influence, presumably deleterious, on government and public opinion. The fetching metaphor implied a need for a grand review not only of the national armament policies but of the very premises of American foreign policy. Was it not in the interest of the complex to exaggerate the dangers of foreign aggression and, hence, of communism?

Not the least troublesome aspect of populist appeals is that they are not susceptible to fine tuning. If President Eisenhower meant to remind the defense community of the primacy of civilian authority, he could have done so with better timing and more aplomb. As it was, his censure of the "military-industrial complex" struck a blow at institutions that supplied the men and the arms without which NATO's Charter would have been another of those scraps of paper that litter the path of diplomatic history.

If President Eisenhower had fault to find with the way the Pentagon did business and the defense industries for exercising undue influence on national politics, then why did he delay disclosing this alarming state of affairs to the last day but two of his presidency? This, too, is a mystery—as is so much about this extraordinary and enigmatic man.

The paradox of America's premier military man warning his countrymen against the influence exerted by the military on American politics and business has agitated American public opinion to this day. To this day, the motives that prompted the president's sweeping indictment and his purpose in making it in his last address to the American people remain controversial. No one could have clarified the issues raised by the president's parting shot more effectively than the president himself. Why, following his departure from office, he chose to remain silent—this, too, is tantalizingly unclear.

Yet, the popular response to the president's rhetorical gambit suffices to tell us, by reflex, where he meant to stand in the remembrance of his countrymen. The proof of the pudding is in the eating. The president, the most popular man of the people in post-World War II America, had come down on the side of the populist option:

> Although war gratifies the army, it embarrasses and often exasperates that countless multitude of men whose minor passions every day require peace in order to be satisfied. Thus there is some risk of its causing, under another form, the very disturbance it is intended to prevent.[5]

Notes

1. Dwight Eisenhower, "Farewell Radio and Television Address to the American People," January 17, 1961, Delivered from the President's Office at 8:30 PM, *Public Papers of the Presidents: Dwight D. Eisenhower, 1960–61* (Washington, D.C.: Office of the Federal Register, 1961), p. 1038.
2. Alexis de Tocqueville, *Democracy in America*, vol. 2, ed. Phillips Bradley (New York: Vintage Books, 1945), p. 284.
3. Ibid.
4. There is no reason why Tocqueville, a meticulous and catholic reader, should not have read Carl von Clauswitz's celebrated treatise *On War*, published as *Vom Krieg*, vols. 1–3 of *Hinterlassenes Werk des Generals Carl von Clauswitz* (Berlin: 1832–34). Tocqueville's interest in German political philosophy was both deep and long-standing, as appears from his correspondence and travels. In 1849

and again in 1854, Tocqueville spent several months in Germany, making the rounds of the famed German universities and meeting some of the great in academia and politics. (He thought Germany favorable soil for the growth of liberal institutions, an error of judgment that he was not alone in making.) As for Clauswitz, his contribution to political philosophy is not confined to his famous axiom that "der Krieg ist nichts als eine Fortsetzung der Politik mit anderen Mitteln." See Raymond Aron, *Clauswitz: Philosopher of War,* trans. Christine Booker and Norman Stone (London: Routledge and Kegan Paul, 1983); originally published as *Penser la guerre* (Paris: Editions Gallimard, 1976). Aron, equally fluent in French, German, and English, also happens to have taken the lead in the "rediscovery" of Tocqueville in the 1960s.

5. Tocqueville, *Democracy in America,* vol. 2, p. 284.

17

Isolationism and the New World Order

Captains of industry tend to bluntness of speech. That is why their observations are apt to reveal more about the state of the American soul, at any given moment, than the more polished, though less concise commentaries of academic students of the nation's inwardness. One such captain of industry, Henry Ford, certainly spoke for American democracy when he said that "history is bunk."[1] Ford, who made more of American history than any other American in this century, hit it on the button. The millions of hard-working Americans who make and use the products of the Ford genius, deem history as being irrelevant to their lives.

And what is that history, in its most general terms? Ancient history was the history of contests between city states, principalities, and empires; modern history—from 1800 to the present—has been the history of the contest of nations and alliances of nations.

This is the history that the American people, had it not been for their greatest leaders' acute sense of history, would have shunned. They wanted to be left alone, to the enjoyment of their ample blessings. This has always been and is still the quintessence of their thought on foreign policy. It has taken enormous effort to budge them, at memorable occasions, from this stance, so simple and so popular.

Even then, the suspension of popular attitudes was never lasting; and Americans always returned to their time-hallowed, commercial preoccupations, as though with finality. None of which, however, is to deny that these commercial preoccupations had made Americans rich enough to afford an unprecedented generosity towards the world, and powerful enough to be generous on their own terms.

During the confrontation of the two superpowers, threatening global war, Americans relaxed their traditional stance to some degree.[2] Now, the appeals of populism and the bureaucratization of life make it likely

109

that American foreign policies will tend to reflect increasingly the priorities of domestic politics, notably the ever-growing demands of the welfare state.

There is in all of this the fatal assumption that winning a war of itself wins the peace to follow. The corollary of that falsehood is that, after a war, the world is safe enough for Americans to neglect it. But Soviet power, and even socialist ideology, has not been the only danger to democracy in our time, just as the principle of autocracy was not the only opponent of democracy when Tocqueville made his famous prediction of the coming contest between America and Russia.

Politically, though, the constituencies for an activist American foreign policy and for its most essential element—the military-industrial complex—lost their bid for their proper share of the nation's resources the day the popular consensus declared the cold war over. It is unlikely that this verdict can be reversed until it is challenged by events so massive as to put in doubt the entire rationale of the now dominant school of thought on foreign policy.

Such a break with the prevailing assumptions about foreign policy would not be without precedent. As a matter of fact, such breaks have occurred several times in the post–World War II history of the United States, at great expense to the American people. "The end of history" notwithstanding, such a break is likely to occur again—at even greater expense to the American people.

Let me concede that this dire prognosis does not jibe with the popular conception of a United States coming to grips with international politics, bestriding the globe as The One Superpower, and creating in its own image a New World Order. My reason for dissenting is that I take a dim view of the call for increased reliance on U.S. diplomacy, in its pursuit of the *national* interest, upon *international* unions (first and foremost, the United Nations). I believe that this alleged internationalism in fact equals *isolationism by another name.* By a stroke of semantic magic, international cooperation under the mantle of the United Nations is supposed to relieve the United States of the burden of its unilateral commitments—not all of them, perhaps, but most.

In effect, the foreign beneficiaries of America's national efforts, at least the solvent ones, are told to raise their contributions to the incidental costs of keeping stability and peace in a new world order. Of course, the savings from this transfer of the global burden, from America's back to the shoulders of the United Nations, are supposed to accrue to the U.S. domestic budget, while the goals of American foreign policy are neatly achieved anyway.

If I deem the assumptions underlying this scenario highly questionable, I do not do so because of the veto power granted by the U.N. Charter to the permanent members. That arrangement merely formalizes the realities of power politics and does not alter them. The Charter leaves it to all members to decide how much or how little of their sovereign power they will delegate to the United Nations.

Here, my concern is rather with the realities that, barring the intervention of cataclysmic events, such as world revolution and a world war, will perpetuate the impotence of the United Nations and preclude its transformation into a New World Order purged of power politics.

In no country have the expectations for a benign alteration of the international system been higher than in America, home of the United Nations. American diplomacy has logic on its side: a universal order is the only viable alternative to universal disorder, armed with all-destructive weapons.

But great expectations, held for a long time, come to be treated as realities. Thus, much of American public opinion tends to reflect on international politics as if its transition to a unitary system had already happened. A myth of the United Nations as the world government has nourished this perilous delusion. There are more true believers in America than in any other U.N. member country.

The indifference and downright cynicism that marks the attitude towards the United Nations of most of its members, except the Western democracies, are not merely the knee jerks of reactionary nationalists and disgruntled diplomats, fearing to be left out from the bureaucracy of the new order. The better part of the United Nations's peoples are skeptical about the responsiveness of the organization to flagrant violations of its own rules. That can be gleaned, at small expense, from what the world press has to say or omits to say about the doings of the United Nations.

The United Nations is a collective of sovereign states, no more than that. In order to have a place in the United Nations, a nation needs to be sovereign. To be sovereign, a nation needs to be subject to no other authority but its own, no matter how benign. For a state to be subject to any other authority signifies the abridgement of its sovereignty—an abridgement of the very condition that gained it admission to the United Nations in the first place.

However unpredictable might be the consequences of the Soviet Union's disintegration, one of these is no longer in doubt: there will be an increase in the number of sovereign nation-states. However unpredictable might be the ultimate outcome of the ideological crisis triggered by glasnost and perestroika, one of its consequences is no longer in doubt: the appeals of nationalism are more powerful than they have ever been.

Thus, the task before American diplomacy is to create a New World Order in which the United States reduces conflict by asserting its position as the leading world power. What else is new about this order as projected by American declaratory diplomacy? Presumably, it is an increase of other concerned nations' share in the management and funding of a stable world order. At a time of rising and virulent nationalism this is the contradiction inherent in the quest for a New World Order that is supposed to be stabler as well as more affordable than the old one.

Notes

1. "History is more or less bunk." See *Chicago Tribune*, May 25, 1916.
2. It was "to some degree" because the American leaders declared the confrontation to be only a "cold" war, its potential consequence, annihilation of the human species, notwithstanding.

18

The End of History

The United States has won the cold war in the sign of an idea: democracy has held its ground against an ideology that, armed with every weapon known to man, sought to subvert it. It has come again to the peoples of East-Central Europe, who, for more than forty years, lived on the other side of the ideological divide. Democracy has also won new ground. And all it has done without a shooting war.

If it is war, the *ultimo ratio* of power politics, that, until now, has made the history of the world, then history is bound to end, for democracies will not go to war against one another.[1] Universal peace has no history—at least not the kind of history that practitioners of power politics have been making. To paraphrase Goethe: Happy are the people who have no history.

The age of the two superpowers has been the Age of Anxiety. Mankind learned to live with the threat of nuclear destruction. Yet, we do not know how great and lasting has been the damage to its psyche from this learning experience. The end of the superpower arms race has been greeted with universal relief. Men have not only been freed of that well-grounded fear; they have been set free to envisage a future order.

In short, the time has come to take stock; the time has come for an intellectual catharsis that gives meaning to these momentous events—the fall of empire, the devaluation of what seemed only yesterday a commanding ideology, and the sweep of liberal democracy across what seemed only yesterday the impregnable heartland of communism. The time has come to unveil a philosophy that explains why what happened had to happen, and why, as Montesquieu put it, all this has been in the "nature of things." The time has come for a philosopher to give the new age its name.

Oswald Spengler gave his age—the age of Europe's fratricidal wars—its name: "the Decline of the West" *(der Untergang des Abendlandes)*.[2] By this name it came to be known to the millions of readers who paid hard cash for the massive volumes in which Spengler explicated his striking metaphor. Though not a few of those who bought his massive publication did not read further than the title, Spengler's somber philosophy captivated the intellectual elite of Europe.

Of course, the response to Spengler's *obiter dicta* was not unanimous. Some of Europe's most distinguished historians denounced Spengler's thesis as a massive intellectual fraud. But this did not diminish its popularity. Nor was it only in Germany that Spengler's *Untergang* became a best seller. Notwithstanding the turgidity of Spengler's prose (which did not ease the translator's task), the *Untergang* achieved international notoriety.

But in Germany proper, the book provided millions with an intellectual home—a *Weltanschauung*—that sheltered them against the despair of defeat and the humiliation of poverty. That Hitler reputedly read Spengler, misunderstood him, and claimed him as his guru, should not be held against the author, who finished the first draft of the work in 1917, long before Germany's regression into the Dark Ages.

Spengler's pessimistic message appealed to a whole generation of Europeans, who had fought the bloodiest and most senseless war in Europe's history and had been left by its stunned leaders with the impossible task of making sense out of the shambles of the greatest and most self-confident civilization to date. Spengler's message of decline and fall, of the uniqueness of culture and the facelessness of mass civilization, got through—loud if not clear—to this star-crossed generation. It also affected the continent's leaders, looking for a philosophical dressing that would make their political salads more palatable to their more discriminating constituencies.

At the current turning point of American history—the end of the cold war and the beginning of new alignments—again there stands a man with a book.[3] The book-buying public has accorded the man and his message a wide and respectful hearing. It was ready to receive them, for "the end of history" is an idea that has never been far from the mainstream of American political thought. After years of benign neglect, the idea has regained the attention not only of the public at large but also of those few whose business is to make history, or to write knowingly about it.

Francis Fukuyama, like Spengler, is an erudite man, steeped in the philosophy of ancient Greece as well as the philosophy of history expounded by Hegel, to whose teaching his fellow German, Marx, owed so great an intellectual debt. Fukuyama stands firmly on the shoulders of this encyclopedic and dogmatic thinker. So did Spengler.

The idea of *The End of History* entered the history of ideas nearly two hundred years ago. In 1806, Hegel contemplated Napoleon's defeat of the Prussian Army at Jena (where he was lecturing), and declared history to have ended. The forces of monarchical absolutism had been routed; the French Revolution that had cast up Napoleon had delivered a mortal blow to the old order of princes, priests, and privilege. From its ruins would rise a new order: the peoples had moved onto the stage of history, and would never leave it again. Hence, no more history!

Fukuyama, contemplating the defeat of communism and the triumph of liberal democracy throughout the Soviet Union and its dependencies, again declared history to have ended. Mankind, redeemed from the history of war and oppression in the name of an absolutist ideology, is now free to attend to its business, which is to make the world more livable. This, exactly, is the purpose of liberal democracy.

Here is not the place to examine the validity of Fukuyama's central thesis.[4] I will only note that after more than sixty years, the West, though badly battered, still refuses to decline. It is unlikely that it will take history less time to prove out the thesis of its own demise.

But while *The End of History* awaits confirmation, its impact on public opinion is not in doubt. The book provides a rationale for those who clamor to cut our defense and foreign affairs budgets. That may explain its manifest popularity in welfarist circles. If postwar retrenchment, an idea usually associated with isolationist conservatism, had been looking for a liberal philosophical warrant it found one in *The End of History.*

Yet the attractive power of Fukuyama's book clearly goes deeper. It resonates in the American psyche like another form of ahistorical predictionism: the literature of science fiction. For sheer quantity, the publications of science fiction are rivalled only by those of biblical exegesis. But great as is the variety of science fiction, and wide as its difference in literary quality from terminal history, the two genres have in common a sovereign disregard of history—the history of the peoples that have lived and still live on this planet.

The figures of science fiction have no nationality: Serb and Croat, Arab and Jew, Xhosa and Afrikaner have ceased to exist. The captains, crews, and passengers of earth-launched space ships might, as a matter of convenience, speak English (the language of most of science fiction's paying readership), but we are not supposed to infer from this their earthly provenience. The sartorial fashions of the people in space are either minimal—the spare cover of athletic nakedness—or the antiseptic smocks of the laboratory.

As for man's predisposition to violence: science fiction divides considerably on this problem. But it is of one mind concerning the scene of battle: if the peoples of science fiction wage war upon one another, they do so in space, and not on the historic battlefields of earthly power politics. They may kill for Mars, but not for Kosovo. Thus ends earthly history; thus ends terrestrial power politics.

In this way, the political innocence of the science-fiction authors meets on common ground with the political sophistication of the terminal historians: both are agreed that the past, since it is no longer prologue, has nothing to teach. There is no precedent for the new order. Relieved of history's burden, mankind is free to fashion the future.

This odd couple—scientific fiction and terminal history—is vastly popular. Both give their respective constituencies what they want. Both cater—unwittingly, one must presume—to the primordial ideology of American democracy in foreign affairs, to wit, isolationism.

Does the end of the cold war mean the end of great power conflict? Has the history of great power politics been closed forever? Since history, as it has been taught ever since Thucydides, has been the history of conflict and power, does the end of power politics mark the end of history *tout court?* Or is this all a passing fancy?

The history of ideas is full of surprises: an idea gains wide public acceptance at a certain time and, at another time, does not. The idea is the same; it is the public that has changed its desires. Having thus changed, the (literate) public searches for a rationale that explains why values heretofore cherished need to be discarded and values heretofore neglected need to be pursued. It is no slight to the earnest men who provide these rationales to say that Americans, when choosing a fresh ideology, are not overly fussy about evidence and logic. It has long been thus. As Tocqueville noted:

> Most of those who live in a time of equality are full of an ambition equally alert and indolent: they want to obtain great success immediately, but they would prefer to avoid great effort.... They flatter themselves that they can delineate vast objects with little pains.... What is generally sought in the productions of the mind is easy pleasure and information without labor.[5]

Notes

1. See the special issue of the *Journal of Peace Research* devoted to this question, vol. 29, no. 4, November 1992.
2. Oswald Spengler, *Der Untergang des Abendlandes*, 2 vols. (1918–1922), published in the United States as *The Decline of the West* (New York: Alfred A. Knopf, 1926–28).
3. Francis Fukuyama, *The End of History and the Last Man* (New York: The Free Press, 1992).
4. See this author's review of *The End of History and the Last Man*, in *Orbis*, Summer 1992, pp. 458–59.
5. Alexis de Tocqueville, *Democracy in America*, vol 2, ed. Phillips Bradley (New York: Vintage Books, 1945), p. 18.

19

The Power of Nationalism

Among the ideologies that, in this century, have moved people to embrace or to fight one another, nationalism is the oldest, the most compelling, and the simplest. It does not tax the intellect of its cohorts; its appeals are simple; the flag is the message; to read it, one need not be literate.

Men do not live by bread alone. Until the Industrial Revolution, the great mass of men were agreed that they could not face alone the precariousness of life and the terror of death. They clasped the hand of God. Belief in God was the spiritual bread that sustained them. By the end of the eighteenth century, this belief that had served to bond human society since time immemorial no longer stood unchallenged. By the beginning of this century, the governments of the advanced industrial states of Europe—England, France, Germany, the Scandinavian countries—were, but for ceremonial anachronisms, secular governments. All of the American states had, virtually on the first day of their independence, legislated the separation of church and state. At the end of World War I, all the succession states of the czarist and the Habsburg empires, respectively, had dissolved irreversibly into congeries of secular states. Never again will a ruler rule by the grace of God.

Yet, if anything is indisputable about the rise and fall of the great ideologies of the nineteenth century that spread their respective messages from Europe to the four corners of the globe, it is that they did not fill the spiritual vacuum created by the evanescence of the great religions. Will nationalism—this is the overarching question—step into the great spiritual emptiness of our civilization that calls itself modern—the Everywhere and the Nowhere of the Global Village?

The idea of nationhood rose from the secularization of European society beginning with the Renaissance; it achieved its apotheosis in the

French Revolution and the French nation-state. A French idea, it swept Europe; it triggered those countermovements that defeated Napoleon's polyglot empire and culminated in the unification of Germany and Italy. At the beginning of this century, nationalism shattered the last surviving forms of dynastic integration, the empires of the Habsburgs, the Romanovs and the Ottoman sultans, and spawned the small nation-states of Central and Eastern Europe. The peacemakers of 1919 wrote the concepts of national self-determination and the equality of nations into the grand settlement of World War I and thus put the finishing touches to what has been called the modern state system.

Virtually from its inception, the arrangement proved neither systematic nor "modern." The forces of nationalism turned destructively upon themselves and confounded those who had meant to base a just and peaceful order upon the satisfaction of national aspirations. Within the framework of the nation-state, the problems of national minorities proved insoluble—and, in the nature of things, will remain forever insoluble. The conditions associated with the idea of the nation-state—an idea of liberal-romantic conception—did not obtain in Eastern Europe, not to speak of non-Western lands.

For the liberal nationalists who, in Europe, manned the barricades of the 1830s and 1840s, and the great liberators of Latin America, "nation" and "humanity" were two sides of the same coin: nationhood was the due of a cultural community democratically governed and mindful of the common interests of mankind.[1] Then, nationalism walked hand-in-hand with democracy.

They are no longer companions. In our times, nationalism, the lowly ideological derivative of a noble idea, is restrained neither by liberal constitutions nor by concern for the common interests of mankind. It is checked only by superior power; it has become the school for violence and dictatorship. It is narrowly parochial; it impedes the exchanges of goods and ideas and thus stunts economic and cultural growth. Nationalism has turned into the greatest retrogressive force of this century. It is now the deadly enemy of democracy.

Nationalism and the USSR

Ever since the middle of the eighteenth century the catch-all net of nationalism has been spreading over the world. It has entangled the collectivist ideologies and choked them in its meshes. As now can be seen, Stalinist communism—the Party and the KGB—was the glue—the only glue—that held together the Soviet state. It herded the peoples under its writ into a huge nation-state, that, though artificial, was compact enough to awe the universe. Its contribution to the welfare of its people, under the brand name of socialism, was conformity in shabbiness. Yet, it prevailed over National-Socialist Germany.

In 1917, Stalin entered Lenin's Soviet government as the commissioner of Nationalities. Until then, his one and only contribution to the literature of Bolshevism had been a slim volume entitled *Marxism and the National Question.* Lenin believed that eventually all nationalities would merge into one and that nationalism would disappear with the evanescence of capitalism. Stalin, making his way on the coattails of the chief, believed what the chief believed—and the chief insisted that the Soviet Union should be a federation of formally equal nations. In the 1920s, various nationalities were granted a measure of self-government under the control of the local communist leaderships. National cultures, even some religions, were allowed to flourish, and all this according to the criteria of nationhood laid down in Stalin's tract published in 1913. It reads as follows:

> A nation is a historically evolved, stable community of language, territory, economic life, and psychological make-up manifested in a community of culture.[2]

It appears to reflect Lenin's thought, for Lenin was not in the habit of allowing his followers to indulge in doctrinaire deviations. It was a notably liberal definition. In the 1930s, Stalin, the autocrat, did not revise it. He reviewed, however, the policies pursued in its name. He drastically reduced the power of the constituent republics. He proceeded to cleanse the Soviet Union ethnically. This, the most brutal of all the brutalities he inflicted upon the Soviet peoples, set the standard for solving the nationality problem by "other means," such as the mass deportation, murder, and forced famine of ethnic minorities.

Not that Stalin contemplated the merger of nationalities, however pliant and decimated, into one. One nationality was to do the merging and to dominate all the others: Russian speech and culture would bond all nationalities into a single Soviet people. Stalin, the expatriate Georgian, metamorphosed himself into Stalin, the Russian nationalist and the even-handed executioner of all non-Russian elites, communist and noncommunist. In the celebration of victory in World War II—the Great Patriotic War—Stalin commemorated only the Russian people, while damning most other nationalities as defectors and traitors.

The contradictoriness of all that Leninism-Marxism has wrought weighed down upon the Party's theoretical statement on nationality and the policies pursued by the Party—read Stalin—in order to solve or, rather, brush aside the problem of nationality. If proof were still needed for the congenital hypocrisy of communism, the fate of the Soviet nationalities provides it. Stalin's *Marxism and the National Question* of 1913 has gone down the drain of malodorous expediency—as has the Soviet constitution of 1936. Both documents take, in theory, a liberal position on the status of nationality. In praxis, the Soviets "solved" the problem of nationality by russification. The nationalities were not to be merged into the classless, uniform society of the Communist Utopia but assimilated to the Russian master race.

For communism—the pristine doctrine straight from the Marxist-Leninist tap—nationalism has always posed a vexing problem that defies a neat rational solution. The proper communist, try as he might, cannot fit the concept of nationhood into the categories of Marxist thought. The Lenins and the Stalins tried. In this they failed. Nationalism has broken the back of the Soviet state. How is it possible to square the putative history of the class struggle with the real history of the nation composed of the elites and the masses, managers and work force, commanders and troops, all marching to the drum beat of patriotism and all prepared—at least metaphorically—to do and to die for the common fatherland?

Nationalism does not discriminate—and cannot discriminate—between classes. It is an adversary ideology—as is Marxism, this being the one characteristic they share. It is a primitive creed. Marx denounced it as false and unscientific. If anything seems clear about the unravelling of the certainties that, once upon a time, sustained the spirit of the peoples under Soviet rule, it is that, as the light of communism has grown dimmer, the light of nationalism has grown brighter and, in some places, effulgently.

Long before the collapse of the Soviet state, the authorities that watched over the teaching of history in public schools, from elementary to university, shifted ground. A succession of textbooks purported to teach the Soviet people how to memorize and how to think about the history of their lands and the world. Soviet historians began to praise the heroic figures of Russian history, such as Ivan the Terrible and Peter the Great, first with faint damn and then, forthrightly, as the makers of the tsarist empire that grew into the vast communist empire at its apogee. Try as they might, the Soviet historiographers failed to catch up with the changes in policy commandeered, with bewildering frequency, at the top of the Party. The avalanche of inconsistencies buried communist scholarship. It did more to discredit communist ideology in the eyes of the Soviet people than did the "contradictions" between dogma and performance. Unwittingly, Soviet scholarship, directed by the state to rewrite Soviet history, triggered a revolution of thinking.

Now, the collapse of the Soviet Union has liberated the nationalities and allowed them to establish themselves as sovereign states, acknowledged as such by the United Nations or diplomatic convention or both. But it has not come near to solving the problems created by russification. For example, at the moment of this writing, the presence of large Russian-speaking minorities in the Baltic states, civilian and military, puts in doubt the effective sovereignty of the three republics. The migration policies of the former Soviet Union, which shuffled and reshuffled the population of the USSR, have altered profoundly the ethnic amalgam inherited from czarist Russia. The result of these manipulations has been to strengthen the Russian minorities embedded in the non-Russian peoples that the czars incorporated in their empire by conquest. Today, the principal beneficiaries of this ethnic logjam are reactionary, antidemocratic, increasingly assertive factions, especially in the Russian and the Ukrainian Republics, both of which are amply endowed with the means of military and (potential) economic power.

Notes

1. Simón Bolívar (1783–1830), called The Liberator, was a South American soldier and statesman who freed Colombia, Venezuela, Ecuador, and Peru from Spanish rule. Futilely, he tried to weld the cultural community of Spanish-speaking Latin America into a single political entity.
2. Joseph Stalin, *Marxism and the National Question: Selected Writings and Speeches* (New York: International Publishers, 1942), p. 12.

20

The American National Interest

The funding of the cold war has been the most costly national effort in the history of the United States. The creation of a New World Order, secure against the dangers faced by the old, will not come at a cost less than that of the heroic enterprise that won America the greatest victory in its history. The pretense that the coming challenge will cost less is at the heart of the argument for a shift of budgetary priorities away from national defense to social services—as though the most fundamental role of government could somehow be put in the balance against those debilitating paternalistic programs Tocqueville warned against. It would be the greatest irony in American history if, in order to feed the unlimited appetite of the welfare state, Americans were to follow the counsels of isolationism garbed as universalism, and opt out of the staggering opportunities that, for a few brief years, will be theirs.

None of this is to assert that a successful American foreign policy is or can be other than a democratic foreign policy in style and substance. Its style must be populist if it is to be a successful foreign policy. Its substance must be populist if it is to be an American foreign policy.

That is to say, the substance of American foreign policy is and cannot be other than this: to secure American democracy against its enemies; to support and defend democratic nations against their enemies; to support pro-democratic forces in countries that have not yet established democratic governments; to shun compromises with nondemocratic governments, even when they claim to be "friendly" to the United States, in the sense of serving some short-term geopolitical interests; and, not least, to advance philosophically the cause of democracy throughout the world.

These are the imperatives of American diplomacy. The defense and advancement of the cause of democracy throughout the world is synonymous with the defense and advancement of American democracy at home. That has always been the sum and substance of American foreign policy. Consistent with its origins, it has been revolutionary, though whether by intent or happenstance is a question to which an answer may never be given. Suffice that American foreign policy has, quite rightly, been seen as revolutionary by the proponents—past and present, domestic and foreign—of what in current diplomatic jargon is called "stability" and what classic diplomacy understood by the term "status quo."

One need not be passionately fond of democracy in all its aspects in order to embrace this foreign policy as a necessity. The point is that the American people *are* passionately fond of democracy, passionate democrats that they are. Given their passion for democracy, Americans are not comfortable when they are forced to contemplate a U.S. foreign policy that does not seem to advance democracy.

They can live with an undemocratic foreign policy so long as the investigative press does not force them to contemplate it: Iran under the shah was an example. But when a populist movement begins to stir in such a country, as it did in Iran, Americans cannot quiet their doubts that the American national interest does not provide a morally valid excuse for siding with undemocratic rulers. There is no point in saying that they should accept it. They don't. And a wise statesman will deal with that and not wish it were otherwise.

Now even so, someone might object, granted that Americans favor democracy, why must they assume responsibility for its coming to be? The reason is to be found in history.

Up until World War I, most educated Europeans and Americans thought that the world was bound to continue on a path of scientific, economic, social, and political progress. They were far from agreed on what that meant—and this, we can now see, should have been a warning sign— but all save for a few eccentrics were convinced that the condition of man was trending upward. In no country was this belief as strongly held as in the United States.

Then came the Great War, the Russian Revolution, the Depression, and the Holocaust—a sequence of events that reduced the idea of mankind's inevitable and benign progress to a macabre joke.

The ambivalence of American democracy about war has skewed American foreign policy ever since its entry in the lists of sovereign states. All sovereign states engage in foreign policy—even if they think that they do not and execrate the idea that they do or should. It is only during the aftermath of World War II—the displacement of Europe as the center of world power by the bipolar system of the superpowers—that the American people learned to live with their status as a world power. A world power, try as it might to pass the buck, cannot help making foreign policy. Gone are the days of the Kellogg-Briand Pact, the Stimson Doctrine, and Armed Neutrality when America was free to choose—or, rather, when Americans could plausibly argue that they were.[1]

As a matter of bleak fact, then, the logic of events leaves the United States, again, as the last best hope of mankind. Among all the nations listed by the Secretariat of the United Nations, it alone can plausibly claim to be the leader of democracy in the world. Europe, some of whose countries have democratic traditions, now has recovered economically, but it is not a political unit. The economically powerful nations of Asia, present and future, lack even Europe's mixed claim to democratic leadership. To abstract the United States's leadership of democratic forces is thus to leave in its place a vacuum such as nature is said to abhor.

Fortunately, the great majority of Americans are agreed that they are irrevocably involved in international politics, and that the initiative is theirs since there is no one else to take it. Now, the controversy has shrunk to how much or how little, and to the priority of the issues that call for American intervention. That most Americans accepted, with good grace, their country's role as a superpower and, now as the only surviving one, does not mean that they rejoice in this awesome distinction, nor have the times made it easier to rejoice.

It is an irony of history, unfathomable and pungent, that the collapse of the Soviet Union should have coincided with a recession of the world economy; that the crisis of leadership in the successor states of the Soviet Union should have coincided with the turmoil of election politics in the major democratic states; and that the unravelling of the bipolar system should have coincided with the proliferation of nationalism worldwide.

In the light of the past, the world can be expected to recover from its economic malaise. Some damage has been done. Crimped by economic shortfalls at home, the major democratic governments' latitude in foreign affairs shrank just at the time when democratic peoples in distress needed their help most. But thus far, the innate commonsense of the American people has not allowed electoral politics to interrupt the continuity of U.S. foreign policy, though here too heavy damage has been done. Too many candidates for electoral office have fallen in with the popular appeals of savings to be garnered from cuts in the national security and foreign policy budget—the "peace dividend."

Nevertheless, what holds for individual men and women, holds for nations, which are—this needs to be repeated endlessly—mere assemblies of individual men and women. Like individual Americans, the American nation needs to embrace its fate as if it had freely chosen it, and most Americans recognize that to lead is America's historic fate. This is a hard truth to swallow for a people that prides itself, quite rightly, on its dynamism—and that wishes to keep out of the commotions of international politics.

If the United States is not to surrender the world to the enemies of democracy, it must pursue foreign policies that will expand rather than contract the reach of its power. Within the global scope of its power, the United States can achieve anything it wishes—except achieve, at least for this next generation, a *stable* New World Order.

Notes

1. For the Kellogg-Briand Pact, see p. 88. The Stimson Doctrine was named for President Herbert Hoover's secretary of state, Henry L. Stimson. Following the Japanese occupation of Manchuria in 1931, he sent notes to Japan and China stating that the United States did not intend to recognize as legally valid any situation brought about by means contrary to the Versailles Treaty.

Part IV

21

Why the Soviet Union Fell

One of the most fateful consequences of the collapse of the Soviet Union is the nearly unanimous agreement of American popular opinion on the cause of collapse. It was, in the generally held view, the malfunction of the Soviet economic system—the empty shelves and the revolt of the consumer—that brought the Marxist-Leninist regime to fall. Thus, the disaster of the communist command economy vindicates the primacy of economics as the mover of history, and the ascendency of the free market points the way to the regeneration and democratization of postcommunist society.

Not only is this assessment of what made the Soviet people demolish the Bolshevik icons wrong, it is also highly dangerous to the good health of all democratic societies.

The economic factor has never been and is not now the motive force of Russian policy, foreign or domestic. In 1914, the economy of czarist Russia was in shambles. It was held together haphazardly by manipulations that defied not only the principles of Adam Smith but also the elementary conceptions of fiscal honesty.

Czarist Russia lived on credit—loans floated in London and Paris that nobody in the high places of finance and government expected Russia to repay and that, as a matter of fact, never were paid off, either by the czarist government or its communist successor. Hundreds of thousands investors the world over—mostly small investors—were relieved by the voracious Russian state and its canny foreign bankers of their life's savings.

Yet, huge as were the borrowings of the Russian state, they did not suffice to pay for the luxuries of the ruling aristocracy or for the world's largest army, possessed of more modern arms than it could effectively handle. The difference between the Russian state's total expenditure and

131

its revenue from domestic sources, including loans and forced labor, was, as it has always been, made up by the spoils of war. Up to our own time, the indispensable item of czarist and Soviet accountancy has been plunder.

Of course, up to our own times, even nations who prided themselves on their dedication to international law and order did not deem it improper to make off with the chattels, public and private, of their defeated foes. Only the evolution of an integrated world market ended this practice. The victors of World War II wisely agreed that they had more to gain from a restoration of the vanquished peoples' economy than from wrecking it.

The only discordant note in this symphony of enlightened mutual self-interest and self-serving liberality was the Soviet Union's vehement insistence on looting the defeated peoples. The war had not yet ended when Moscow began to plunder Japanese Manchuria and the Germanies as well as the East European territories occupied by the Red Army.

Now, nearly fifty years have elapsed since World War II. But to this day, Russia exacts tribute, in the guise of reparations, from its European satellites. Parts of the Russian army are even housed and fed at the expense of free Germany. More astounding still, free Germany has agreed to build, at German expense, and within the Soviet Union proper, housing complexes that will accommodate the veterans of the Red Army returning from occupation duty. The total of these exactions is likely to run into the tens of billions of dollars. And the end is not yet. The states of Eastern Europe might now be free and sovereign. But the remainder of the Red Army, stationed abroad, will, for years to come, enjoy their hospitality, enforced by treaty and at staggering costs.

Directly or indirectly, the Soviet Union's revenue from plunder accrued to the benefit of the one and only sector of the Soviet Union's economy that could claim a high efficiency and uninterrupted growth rate, namely, war-oriented industry. Without this contribution, even this exception from the general regression of Soviet industrial productivity would have been impossible.

But here is not the place to pass judgement on the ethics of Soviet economic policies, at home and abroad. The losses to the Soviet Union from World War II were enormous, though probably not greater than those inflicted upon the Russian people by decades of Stalinist misrule. Suffice that the collapse of the Soviet economic system has opened a new chapter in the history of Russia and her quondam satellite states and, for that matter, in world history.

There is good reason for the capitalist states to assist the quondam Soviet peoples in exploiting their vast natural and intellectual resources and joining the community of the advanced economic states. There is, however, equally good reason for not mistaking the economic problems of postcommunist Russia—largely posed by the liquidation of the communist system—for the economic problems that confront the Western democratic states.

The Russian economy has never been even faintly like ours. Russian economic policy under czardom and communism has been the acquisition of wealth by state power. The private sector accumulated its wealth by the grace of the state. Capitalism throve by the dispensation of the czars who, whenever it pleased them, could revoke it—and did. Private capitalism—be it in the sense of Adam Smith, be it in the sense of Karl Marx—never had a legal basis in Russia. Whatever difference there was between the Czar Nicholas's and Stalin's conception, respectively, of the capitalist system was a matter of style rather than substance.

To be sure, there were rich men in czarist Russia—bankers and industrialists—who, by all appearances, practiced the arts of capitalism. But if capitalism entails private property, then these "capitalists" of czarist Russia were not true members of the species: the right to own property, like all rights, derived from the will of the autocrat.

The economic system of czarist Russia, in so far as it simulated Western capitalism, was more productive and humane than its dogmatic and, by a broad margin, more brutal, successor. But this did not alter the fact that the peoples of Russia under czardom and then communism have been kept in ignorance of capitalist economics and taught to despise the little they knew about it. That this circumstance has not been brought home to the public of the Western democracies, forthrightly and emphatically, apparently derives from a generic "weakness" of democracy— the penchant of democratic governments to follow public opinion rather than lead it, to tell the people what they like to hear rather than what they ought to hear, no matter how unpleasant the message. American democracy, too, might be in need of a glasnost of its own.

The cardinal assumption of American foreign policy toward Russia needs to be made explicit: the assumption that the dissolution of the Soviet empire was caused by the collapse of its economy. If this assumption holds, then economics will determine the order, political and social, that will succeed to the defunct Soviet state, as well as the relationships among one another of the Soviet Union's successor states. The fortunes of democracy in these ex-Soviet states will be contingent on the rise of average living standards, and, hence, on the creation of a capitalist economy. Then, too, American policy towards the ex-Soviet states must be supportive of the latter's efforts towards this fundamental alteration—not reform—of the expiring Soviet system.

In brief, the model for the new society that will take the place of the communist system will be no other than our own. The priorities of that new society will be the same as those that govern American democracy. The ex-Soviet peoples will be driven by the same, predominantly economic, urges that have shaped American society. The average Russian will have the same wants as the average American. Both will be alike—except for some minor differences of speech and diet. If the assumption is correct, American policy should be guided by an identity of aspirations that joins all peoples and overrides national peculiarities.

But this diagnosis of the causes of the Soviet Union's collapse and the prescription for a grand economic rescue action, enthusiastically welcomed by the leaders of the ex-Soviet states, are in essence informed by the isolationist-universalist ideology pledged to liberate America from the bondage of power politics. *Homo politicus* yields to *homo economicus,* destined to conquer the world without force other than the attraction of the market.

Unfortunately for this policy, however, Soviet man was not *homo economicus.* Neither was his forebear, the subject of the czar. Karl Marx, the economist, was right to reject Russia as the proper place for the consummation of his proletarian revolution. Not only did the Russian working masses fail the test of class consciousness, but the Russian economy had not yet completed the progression from feudalism to capitalism.

Have the years since the demise of Marx succeeded in creating a truly modern Russian society and people? We know the attempt has failed abysmally. The "New" Russians are no more like us than the "Old." Their attitudes towards life and death are not those of the American people. Mute and sullen, ill-housed and ill-fed, the Russian people did not protest the Stalinist holocaust, the murder of twenty million compatriots. Yet, this same people rose in 1940 to the defense of the motherland, their feats of heroism and selfless patriotism saving not only their country but their murderous leaders. And then, they slipped back into the valley of submissive discontent. Whatever else they are driven by, it does not appear that the Russian people are driven by the urges that animate *homo economicus*.

Thus, the question of what caused the collapse of the Soviet Union is a crucial one. It is crucial not only for the future of the Commonwealth of the Independent States but also for America and America's fellow democracies. On the answer will depend the choice of not only the remedial policies by the successor states to the USSR, but also the responsive policies of the Western democracies.

The issue is still in doubt—and will remain in doubt for a long time. The great debate has only begun. One answer, more than a little unfashionable, should not be overlooked: that the democratic West set out to bring down the Soviet Union, and succeeded; that the collapse of the Soviet Union was, in William Hyland's words, the final "vindication of the classic containment theory."[1]

Containment

The "containment" of Soviet power was never supposed to be a passive policy, as President Ronald Reagan understood. It aimed not only at blocking Soviet expansionism but at the destruction, physical and moral, of the Soviet empire.

It was, from the start, a policy of engagement in the struggle for freedom of all the peoples under the yoke of communism. It aimed at the erosion of Soviet military power by eroding that military's economic base. The policy certainly would have succeeded more quickly, to the benefit of millions at home and abroad, had it been pursued more vigorously and more consistently.

But, consistent or not, the policy worked. It was the exhaustion of the Soviet economy that forced the Soviet Union out of the arms race. Once the leaders of the Soviet Union recognized that they had lost this race, perestroika and glasnost followed as night follows day.

That this was brought about by the Soviet leaders' and Party's conversion to liberalism is an imaginative idea—as imaginative as a production of Hamlet without the Danish prince. The failure of Western statesmen to publicly nail down the causation of the cold war's denouement—because they wish to spare the sensitivities of the East's new leaders, or because they wish to appease accommodationist factions in Western politics, who are unforgiving for having been proven wrong—has not been helpful to American diplomacy in seeking to gain the support of the public for coherent foreign policies.

After all, if it was not the classic containment policy that has forced the Kremlin to change its mind, then exactly what caused it to abandon its forty-year attempt at global hegemony? Could it not be that this attempt exhausted the economic resources of the Soviet Union as well as those of its Warsaw Pact allies, and that the extravagances of the Soviet military-industrial complex bankrupted the communist empire? Could it not be—indelicate as might be the thought—that the United States won the arms race?

In particular, could it not be that the Kremlin was impressed by the steadfastness of the United States and its allies when the Reagan administration succeeded in deploying the intermediate-range Pershing II missiles, in the face of Soviet taunts and threats? To be sure, the deployment of those missiles merely closed a large gap between the intermediate-range capabilities of NATO and those of the Soviet Union, a gap that had existed long before the NATO allies agreed in 1977 on a program for improving their, in part obsolescent, intermediate-range missile force. Clearly, the Soviets did not reappraise their economic and foreign policies because they had suddenly awakened to a novel threat to the strategic equilibrium posed by NATO's deployment of weapons systems, the equivalents of which they themselves possessed in plenty. Yet, it is far from unreasonable to suppose that the changes in Moscow, which began as perestroika and which then became unstoppable, were indeed prompted by the Kremlin's realization that it could not hope to break down the military and political barrier of containment, export the USSR's chronic internal crisis into the capitalist world, and coerce conquered peoples into subsidizing its rotting economic system.

As Robin Ranger puts it in a brief but admirable explanation of the Soviet Union's collapse:

> Under [President] Reagan the U.S. accelerated the development and deployment of a new generation of high-technology weapons whose effectiveness was demonstrated in the Gulf War. The Soviet military leadership then found that the nation's economy could not support the development and deployment of comparable weapons systems, and so Soviet margins of military superiority were reduced. The So-

viet leadership also found that President Reagan, Prime Minister Thatcher, and other allied leaders refused to be intimidated, especially as the U.S. and allied military position improved.[2]

President Reagan would be the last to claim that he was "the right man at the right time" to accomplish this victory. Certainly, the achievement was not his alone. Nevertheless, it was the policies of his administration that forced the issue. It was the build-up of forces during the years of his presidency and the consistency of his foreign policies that broke the back of a regime that had nothing better to offer its people than a stagnant ideology and the lifestyle of the *nomenklatura*. The Soviet Union fell because we deprived it of its power to intimidate abroad and, hence, to intimidate at home.

Notes

1. Robert Strausz-Hupé, "A Vindication of Containment," review of *The Cold War,* by William G. Hyland, *Orbis,* Summer 1992, p. 156.
2. Robin Ranger, "Special Report, Military Affairs, The Soviet Military Collapse," *1993 Britannica Book of the Year* (Chicago: Encyclopaedia Britannica, Inc., 1993), p. 233.

22

The Former Soviet Union Today

At the time Tocqueville made his famous prediction about the eventual clash of America and Russia, the latter was a monarchy. Tocqueville's prediction came true when Russia was a communist state. Does this mean that the prediction's success was mere chance? Not at all. Tocqueville's terse forecast accommodated both the religious-geopolitical imperialism of czarist Russia and the ideological-geopolitical imperialism of communist Russia because they were essentially similar.

I say this realizing full well that Marx considered Russia the country least likely to consummate the transition from feudalism to capitalism and, hence, the least likely place for the proletarian revolt against the bourgeoisie—both proletariat and bourgeoisie accounting, in his time, for a portion of the Russian population much smaller than the portion of these classes in the industrial countries of Europe. In Marx's day, the Russian people were still closer to the soil, economically and emotionally, than were the Western peoples. In Marxist parlance, the Russian proletariat was too weak to wage the *klassenkampf*—the battle of the classes.

But the communist revolution did in fact begin in Russia, not because the country was "ready" for it according to the obscure dialectics of Marx, but because (as Tocqueville had realized) Russia had an autocratic soul. Czarism was the rule of the anointed despot before whom every subject, be he prince or serf, was equal. Likewise, under Soviet communism, every member of the Party was the equal of every other member of the Party, equal in his submission to the dictatorship of the proletariat. Mikhail Gorbachev's authority did not issue from the free choice of the members of the Party, not to speak of the free choice of the Russian people. It was exercised by decree; it was not consecrated by the vote of the members of the Party, not to speak of the vote of all the

Russian people. Comrade Gorbachev ruled as autocratically as did the czar. He did not claim to rule by the grace of God. He did claim to derive his authority from the Marxist-Leninist dogma—a source as mysterious as the will of God by which the czar claimed to rule.

The analogy explicated above—the old and the modern autocrat—might invest the former secretary-general with more power than he had in fact. He shared power—no one knows how much—with his colleagues in the Politburo, with the chiefs of the restive army, and the chiefs of the omnipresent secret police, rivals of the Party hierarchy. But then too the czarist army, as well as the czarist secret police, were not always as blindly subservient to the czar as they professed to be.

Thus, the differences between the two autocracies were minor. The successive secretaries-general did not seem to have felt quite as secure in their supreme rule as did the anointed czars, but the resemblances were close, shockingly close. Siberian exile under the czars and life in the Gulag at the discretion of the secretaries-general have been, for millions of Russians, the same thing. What the czars gave to their subjects, the czars could take away; what the secretaries-general gave, the secretaries-general could take away.

Of course, rule by czar or secretary-general was not the same at all times. There were reforms galore under the czars, and reforms, hailed as momentous, were launched by the last of the secretaries-general. But the reforms had this in common: they were granted by the supreme ruler to his subjects. They were not won on the barricades or in the chambers of Parliament. They were the ruler's gift to his subjects, equal with one another before him in their lack of power. And this made a tremendous difference in the effects of the reforms: absolute power is said to corrupt; so does absolute lack of power.

Here, I remorselessly press the point, for all of our policies towards the Commonwealth of Independent States revolve around the degree to which their policies reflect the will of the people. Yet, at present, the articulate popular will in those states is not strong enough to shape and ratify what the Russian and other Commonwealth politicians have wrought.

At some future time, there may be such a popular will. But not if the new leaders fail to replace dictatorial authority—on all levels, national and local; on the factory floor and in the schoolroom alike—with authority freely chosen by, and responsible to, the people. Without that, the leaders' professed commitment to free speech, free markets, free travel, and the rule of law at home and abroad will not stand.

The issue is still in doubt. But, if there is one popular consensus in post-Soviet society, it is that the battle for democracy remains unfinished.

The new rulers, having bestowed upon their stunned countrymen the blessings of democracy, face immense difficulties of application, as they were bound to. Unavoidably, the transition from the old system to the new has been fraught with civil strife and economic regression. The principal reason for this has to do with what communist society was: the rule of mediocrity.

The USSR did not lack men capable at their calling, ingenious and exceptional in their achievement. Not all who labored for the Party, and submitted loyally to its flawed dogmas, were fools or toadies. Mendacious though the leadership was, not all members of the Soviet Union's immense state bureaucracy were liars or lied to themselves in their ritual devotion to the Party. Not all the motivations of the Party politicians were ignoble or lacking in civic idealism. Consequently, it should come as no surprise to the Commonwealth's new won friends in the high places of Western capitalism that many communists genuinely despise them. The CEO is not yet—and might never be—a Russian cult figure. He is not that in the West.[1]

Yet, if the selfless Stakhanovite tradition had its adherents in the Soviet Union, no one will pretend that it was these men and women to whom the mass of bureaucrats looked for its role model. To the more typical bureaucrat, what the communist social order offered was an attractively undemanding way of life. Shabby as the bureaucratic setting might have been, it was secure. The expectations of the eighteen million bureaucrats that ministered to the Soviet Union[2]—from the great hierarchs down to the vendors of postage stamps—were not quite the same as their opposite numbers in the Western bureaucracies, public and corporate.

That explains (and suffices to explain) the failure of Soviet communism to tap the latent resources, intellectual and material, of the world's largest country—and deliver on its promises to its people. The failure of Soviet agriculture to feed its people adequately—not to speak of producing grains for export as czarist Russia managed to do with ease—was the most humiliating one among all humiliations communist mismanagement has piled on the Soviet people.

Achievers in America might be only a small minority of the population, but they are numerous enough to generate the upward propulsion of the U.S. economy that allows it to keep pace with the rising expectations of the country's people. In the Soviet Union, this thrusting contingent did not exist, for it was through the conduits of the Party that the clever and ambitious rose to the places of power and the enjoyment of perquisites that, rather than nominal salaries, were the real rewards of their jobs.

In a reforming Russia, wedded to efficiency and transparency, the former high bureaucrat, quondam member of the *nomenklatura,* has much to lose now that his ideological claim to a powerful job has vanished. His distance from the average bureaucrat is still as wide as that between the CEOs of the *Fortune* 500 and the salaried corporate bureaucracy that does their bidding—a long way to fall. Yet, others, too, feel they have much to lose. At lower levels, with fewer perquisities, job security assured the Party of its members' loyalty and assured the state of its employees' subservience, no matter how grudging.

Thus, whatever the motive of the Soviet bureaucrat, his admission to gainful employment depended upon proof of Party loyalty plus a modicum of competence, certainly not professional excellence. If the Party found the employee wanting in compliance with communist rote, his dismissal followed; excellence could not save him. This two-track job qualification—the skill needed for the job itself and proven fluency in Marxist-Leninist dogma—made certain that the job holder be obedient rather than skilled and industrious.

For an ever-rising part of the population, this system—with its promise of relatively undemanding security—had its attractions, and not only among those who were forced to endure it. For decades, the Marxist-Leninist model enthralled large numbers of the people in the most advanced and prosperous states of Europe, such as France and Italy.

I press this point regarding the psychological dimensions of the Soviet system, because it is only a massive shift in the political consciousness of the Russian people that will allow reform to happen and arouse the Russian people from their torpor. Until this shift occurs, all analogies—representative institutions, theirs and ours; civilian control of the military, theirs and ours; freedom of speech, theirs and ours; budgetary controls, theirs and ours; and, last but not least, the temper of political man, Russian and American, are false.

It is this fundamental political-psychological incompatibility of the two nations—in the New World, America, having forged a new republican state, defeated its enemies abroad, matched civic equality with civic liberty; and, in the Old World, Russia, benumbed by the rule of the autocrat accountable to no one—that Alexis de Tocqueville was first to perceive and to state.

A shift in the consciousness of the former Soviet peoples seems to have begun, forced upon them by the consequence of the communist system in practice. But, to understand that shift, one must ask why it did not occur earlier. For instance, one must ask why, living amid Third World conditions, they tolerated for seventy years, and without an audible whimper, the Soviet Union's investment of (at least) one-quarter of its gross domestic product in the technology of military and political warfare?

They did so because they found the case made for the system by their rulers plausible, not because they lacked information about politics or the sophistication needed to evaluate it. The average Soviet citizen spent more time listening to and debating information on world politics than the average American. His government saw to that by supplying abundant information and expert guidance for evaluating it.

The average Soviet citizen may have lacked that instant information, transmitted electronically, that is available to Americans. But the Soviet media made up for this deprivation by unremitting didactic guidance. Much, though not all, of the information supplied by the state monopolies of communications was wrong, if not mendacious, and all of the comment was doctrinally skewed. That does not mean, however, that the Soviet citizenry lacked enough sophistication to read between the lines: as long as the Soviet people remained besotted by Marxist-Leninist doctrine, even the grossest discrepancies of information received and the facts withheld by the subservient media (most of which seeped down by various and countless channels to the Soviet public) did not shake the Soviet people's faith in the rightness and goodness of the communist regime.

In the end therefore, it was not lack of information about the state of the world, but the stark realities of a nation-wide economic breakdown, and the Soviet rulers' abdication of authority, for all to see, that destroyed the Soviet people's faith in Marxist-Leninist doctrine and, with it, the Soviet state.

U.S. Policy

The shrinkage of communist power has triggered centrifugal forces, heretofore repressed, in almost all the states along the rim of the Soviet Union. Most of these states will have to come to grips with the multi-ethnic issues that, before World War II, made them such easy prey of the Nazi-fascist predators. Since then, these divisive issues have increased in numbers and intensity.

Although it is not yet clear where the succession states are going, their respective governments need to be assured of the West's assistance in transforming their economic system and maintaining their territorial integrity.

The most effective rebuttal of the naysayers (who profess to see behind the fair countenance of Russian democracy the specter of totalitarian reaction) is to concede the ambiguity of the reforms achieved thus far, but to ask: ambiguous or not, is there any sure alternative to the incumbent regimes? If there is not, then the West has no choice other than to support the democratic reformers and stand clear of the internal conflicts that threaten the unity of the Commonwealth.

Such, at the time of this writing, seems to be the policy of the United States. As long as now unforeseeable traumatic events do not upset the balance of forces crafted by the reformers, this will continue to be U.S. policy.

Notes

1. Thus, Irving Kristol says: "Bourgeois society is without doubt the most prosaic of all societies.... It is a society organized for the convenience and comfort of common men and women, not for the production of heroic, memorable figures." Irving Kristol, *Reflections of a Neoconservative* (New York: Basic Books, 1983), p. 28. Evidently, though he is the author of *Two Cheers for Capitalism,* Kristol does not find capitalist leaders from Commodore Vanderbilt to William Gates either heroic or memorable.

2. See *The Current Digest of the Soviet Press,* "Ministries' Staffs Cut, Enterprises Go Up," vol. xli, no. 10 (April 5, 1989), p. 8. *The Current Digest* provides a condensed text of an *Izvestia* story from March 7, 1989, reporting on the State Statistics Committee Reports, and entitled "Where Are the Managers and How Many of Them Are There?" In a table labelled "Number of Employees in the Administrative System," the line for "Managerial personnel of enterprises and organizations" gives a 1985 figure of 14,840,000 and a 1988 figure of 14,962,000. There is an asterisk for this line, however, which leads to a footnote reading,

"Not including security personnel, messengers, stenographers, typists and other employees excluded from the standard list of managerial personnel. Counting these categories, the number of managerial-apparatus employees totaled 17.7 million in 1985."

23

The Primacy of Europe

Thus far, geography, tradition, and mutual self-interest have oriented American foreign policy, first and foremost, toward Europe. Even in the age of space exploration, terrestrial geography has remained a constant in international relationships. If history teaches any lesson, it is that it does not pay to argue with geography. The Atlantic Ocean does not separate America from Europe: it joins them. The direct investment of Europe in America is far greater than that of any other region; and the direct investment of America in Europe is far greater than its direct investment in any other region.[1]

Yet, geography and economics are but two elements and, historically, not the most important ones, in the American-European connection. The traffic in ideas, the ties of culture, the products of the creative arts, the shared memories of great things done, and the intimacy of countless interpersonal relationships are far more important. These are the living stuff of the American-European connection. These are the reason that, in both World Wars, the primacy of Europe in American foreign policy and American strategy was axiomatic.

If the primacy of Europe in American foreign policy were merely a matter of geopolitics and trade it would prove as perishable as all the works of pragmatic statesmanship from the Treaty of Westphalia to the Treaty of Versailles to the Pact of Yalta. It has been the American-European consensus on ultimate values—on the rights and the wrongs of human conduct in society—that, without the dispensation of treaties and protocols, has kept America's European connection green.

In this way, the links that today forge the ties between America and Europe are like the links that staved off a general European war in the hundred years between the Napoleonic Wars and World War I. The diplomacy of the nineteenth century was what it had always been since the rise of the nation-state, to wit, secretive, tricky, unscrupulous, and unashamedly self-seeking. The result of this shocking amorality in the pursuit of the national interest was a spate of local wars, but no universal conflagration.

How, then, did the World Wars of the twentieth century come about? The answer is simple: the actors on the stage of world politics were no longer the same, and they no longer read from the same script.

In the nineteenth century, the actors and supporting cast were the scions of the hereditary aristocracy and the bourgeois leaders of high finance, the society of high birth and the society of great wealth. Whatever might have been the cracks in this amalgam, it was held together by a powerful consensus on values—how the good life should be lived in civilized society and how its members should behave toward one another.

Not so surprisingly, it was Britain, the strongest member of this consensus, that had devised—and stood ready to enforce—the conventions, explicit or unspoken, that sustained it. The Protestant ethos of work and the code of the English gentleman set the rules of the world market. On the Lord's Day, business came to rest.

Today, the hopes for a general European peace rest with the European Union (EU)—the community of peoples that have warred upon each other ever since the fall of the Roman Empire. Undoubtedly, the Union is Europe's greatest postwar achievement. But, lest we forget, many features of the Union are identical with those of Europe before World War I, and some of the freedoms enjoyed by the Europeans in the age of the Long Peace have not been restored as yet. Not the least among these is the right to move across borders (except for the Russians) without documents of identification and permits to settle and to work for a living wherever work could be found.

The bureaucracy of the EU is hard at work to relax its controls on these freedoms. More likely than not, the EU of the future will be internally as free of barriers to the movement of people and goods as the respective nations were before they joined up. The idea of European economic unity is prevailing over the idea of nationalism. However, the creation of Europe is not stirring the optimism about the future progress of humanity that great international achievements once engendered.

Nor has the enthusiasm of individual Europeans about their new home run away with them. Whatever might be their feelings towards it, Europatriotism is not among them. The EU has not yet asked its peoples to pledge their lives and fortunes in its defense, and, but for a small minority, Europeans would be deeply shocked by such a request. A surprisingly large number of Europeans would still do battle for their respective national homes. So long as the EU remains merely a pragmatic convenience, Europe will remain a convenient abstraction.

Fortress Europe?

The idea of the supranational European market has a supranational constituency, namely, Europe's consumer society. Such a consumer society is outward looking: it will shop wherever desirable goods are on offer at the lowest cost. And, of course, the laws of the market govern U.S.-EU economic relationships, as well as intra-EU relations. Thus, America need not fear European protectionism as long as European consumers—who happen to constitute Europe's political majority—desire American produce at a cost less than other imported goods of the same kind.

Ironically, therefore, the less "economic" and more "national" Europe becomes, the greater the danger to America's relationship with the EU. So long as members of the EU pursue unity largely in order to pursue free trade and the free movements of people, they are likely to pursue similar policies with other free states. However, if Europeans begin to think of themselves as one people, united amid a world of alien peoples, the EU will tend to harden into a protectionist and even nativist state.[2]

But will not American-European trade itself guarantee that such xenophobia does not turn trans-Atlantic?

The idea that peoples need do no more than trade with one another in order to understand one another better and, in the fullness of time, to like and esteem one another, is not the least among the many pernicious ideas about international relations now current in academe and the press. Gratifying as the thought may be to the American-European trading community, philosophy and history demonstrate that trade does not necessarily strengthen the bonds of friendship.

Trade is a rigorously selfish activity. Good feelings between the trading parties are optional; they are not necessary. If it were not so, the British and the Germans should, in 1914, have been firm friends. Yet, overnight, they stopped trading with one another and started to shoot at one another. It seems that a critical factor was missing from the equation.

Fortunately, the tree of American-European concord is today as sturdy as ever. But, like all organic things, it needs feeding and pruning. Its needs must not to be taken for granted. Our memory spans need to be extended beyond the last political issue that, for a week, has displaced another issue in the public's view—and in another week will be forgotten.

Notes

1. U.S. Department of Commerce, *Survey of Current Business,* June 1993, pp. 51-54.
2. So far, European xenophobic nationalism, as a political force, has been confined to the extreme margins of European politics, though the nationalist opposition has been gaining ground, especially in France, burdened as that country is by the enigmatic bequest of Charles de Gaulle. Fortunately, such nationalism has been plagued by the contradiction of seeking a Europe united in opposition to the foreigner "without," as well as a nation united in opposition to the foreigner "within."

24

NATO

Contemporary Europe, America's junior partner in the founding of the New World Order, is not the Europe of forty years ago, which, under the wing of American power, developed its unitary institutions and unprecedented wealth. Its physical environment has changed—in some places beyond recognition. The tenor of political debate has changed—in some places stridently. Europe senses her power, political as well as economic. The enfeeblement of communist Europe has been democratic Europe's gain in strength. The Soviet debacle has raised Europe to the rank of a world power.

This "new" Europe, the Europe of "mixed" economies, of dominant state bureaucracies, and of widening political ambitions challenges the mettle of American statecraft and the ingenuity of its executive arm, American diplomacy. Never has Europe been so near to America as she is now; never have the institutions—from providential welfare state to supermarket—looked more alike than they do now. It is the centerpiece—the will to do great things together and to "silence immediate needs for the view of the future"—that is lacking, while the slide towards uniformity and centralized bureaucratization is gutting the vital sources of the American-European relationship.

Thus far, American and European public opinion has welcomed America's invitation to the New World Order with cordial approbation and a lengthy list of reservations. The latter leave unresolved the issue of burden sharing, notably the willingness of NATO's European member states to compensate for the reduction of the U.S. forces deployed in Europe. So far, the Allies have not agreed on the "savings"—cuts of defense budgets—to be garnered from the dissolution of the Warsaw Pact. Does the remainder of the Soviet military potential, most of it now based in the Federal Republic of Russia, still pose a threat to NATO Europe?

If it does not, then the problem facing the Alliance is how to liquidate itself and release its members from their pledges to their common defense. Then, there would be no longer a burden to be shared. Then, American-European relations would center upon trade between the two gigantic consumer societies, who are bent upon increasing the wealth and comfort of their peoples.

The prospects are pleasing: America and Europe, relieved of the burden of defense, settling their differences on government subsidies to select industries and imposts on select commodities. It should be relatively easy. Never has the web of American and European corporate relationships been as dense as it is now. Never have the Atlantic democracies been so close to economic union.

But the Atlantic community is not today closer to political union than it was a generation ago; it is less close, partly because of the cold war's end, partly because of the EU's rise.

Whatever political unity the Western democracies have found, they have found it under the roof of NATO. The end of NATO would be the dismantlement of the military alliance of the Atlantic states. It would also spell the end of the one and only political institution of the Atlantic community. Since its inception, NATO has been more than a military coalition, although less than a confederation.

At its inception, NATO promised a closer union. That is why, ever since the day of its creation, NATO's enemies from without and within have labored unceasingly to bring about its dissolution. Their target has not been the economic union of Europe, but the political-strategic integration of American and European power, the hard core of the American-European connection. To preserve this core and to build on it should be the overarching purpose of American diplomacy.

Democracy requires predictability and, hence, stability, and, hence, security. This sense of security, nurtured by democratic fellowship, liberated Europe from the hounding fear of Soviet aggression and civil war, thus freeing the spirit of enterprise that is the motive force of the open market. First things need to be put first: without a sense of security, the EU would not exist. The founders of the EU (then called the European Community), Robert Schuman and Konrad Adenauer, understood and embraced this primacy of the defense of Europe.[1] It is no longer certain that their heirs in Brussels still do.

The Anchoring of West Germany

The overarching purpose of the United States's postwar German policy has been to seal West Germany irrevocably into the fellowship of Western democratic nations. The purpose was achieved. The outcast from international society was metamorphosed into the leader of the European democracies and the most powerful ally of the United States. This feat would have been impossible without the transformation of German society from the ground up—a transformation that eluded the Weimar Republic, and the lack of which condemned the German people to the repetition of their paranoid history.

The society of the *Bundesrepublik* is of American make, the handiwork of a small band of creative American politicians and legions of American pedagogues, some in uniform, charged with the re-education of the German nation. This claim of copyright, I concede, does not quite jibe with the official version, German and American, of Germany's postwar history. It suffices, however, to explain the smooth and the rough of the American-German connection.

The "Americanization" of Germany is a metaphor and, like all metaphors, an oversimplification. "Americanization," if the term means anything, means a method of producing things and a habit of enjoying things thus produced, living tranquilly under laws legislated by the people and debating these laws freely and vociferously. By these criteria, Germany is unmistakenly "Americanized." It bears the indelible marks of its almost fifty years' cohabitation with American democracy—its power, its way of life, its idiosyncrasies, and its good humored indulgence. If this were not so, the "economic miracle" and the rise of German power would be an inexplicable historic accident, and Germany would still sit on Europe's bench of the accused.

Nevertheless, the history of democracy in Germany is brief. Depending on whether the Weimar Republic is counted in as a healthy specimen or excluded as a congenital cripple, democracy in Germany is a matter of forty or sixty years. "Americanization" has compressed and accelerated the process of "democratization." Will this instant democracy endure as American power and influence recede from Europe? How deeply are the Germans and, especially, the German young committed to Germany's young democracy?

The possibility of Germany seeking again to master Europe and so reverse the verdict of total defeat is said to disquiet, fifty years after the event, the peoples Hitler conquered. The loudest and most prestigious voices warning against German recidivism have been French. France has good reason to keep alive the memories of Nazi iniquities, for, among the European peoples enslaved by the Nazis, France suffered most deeply her degradation. She ceased to be a world power—and she will never again be a world power—notwithstanding her ceremonial place among the permanent members of the U.N. Council.

This is not merely a matter of cold statistics. France's sense of insecurity vis-à-vis democratic Germany, its insistence that the latter's military potential be hedged in by a tight system of international controls, betrays a lack of that matter-of-fact self-assurance that is the first prerequisite of great-power status. De Gaulle's retirement marked the end of a great illusion; in this, the most cost-conscious age in history, grandeur lost cannot be recovered by rhetoric no matter how magnificent. French foreign policy, though not French posturing, reflects the cold realities of life as a second-rate power—a power that cannot afford and cannot enforce global policies of its own conception.

France, like all powers that cannot stand alone, has sought salvation in coalition diplomacy—making up for the inadequacy of her own power by alignments with other nations. Today, because of the European Union, France need not fear to face alone a resurgent Germany. Not coincidentally, the outstanding architects of the EU were Frenchmen, Schuman and Jean Monnet.[2] Submerging Germany in a United Europe has been the quintessential idea of French foreign policy. The time for it has come: Germany, with the solemn approbation of France, has taken her place in a democratic Europe; her productive energies are harnessed to the development of an all-European economy; and, most important, the German people are happily committed to opulence without grandeur, to the works of peace rather than the production of high-tech weaponry.

The Incorporation of East Germany

Or so it has been until recently. In the last few years, the conditions that fostered European harmony, and should have laid to rest French doubts about the depth of Germany's commitment to European goodfellowship, have changed. The balance of power *within* Europe has been upset by East Germany's return to the national fold. The East Germans have not shared their Western brothers' educational experience. "Americanization" stopped at the Wall.

The East Germans are predominantly Prussian. The communist regime cultivated deftly the mythology of the Prussian state. Communist propaganda claimed East Germany's affinity with the Prussia of Frederick the Great, a talented despot, and the East German army goose-stepped with that truculence that made "Prussian" a byword for militarism and aggression. But these were the convulsions of a bankrupt regime.

The absorption by the opulent, democratic, decentralized German Federal Republic of the ragged fragments of the police state that called itself mendaciously the German Democratic Republic has been a gigantic enterprise. It has been a conquest by love, not violence. It now proceeds at a steady pace. It attests the vigor of German democracy. "Americanization" is spreading to the lands beyond the Wall. With the successful consummation of this process, democracy will again stand firm not only in Germany but in Europe. With its failure, the European Union must fall.

Thus, those who still fear a revival of the Germans' martial spirit should do what they can to make the enterprise of unification succeed. Certainly, it should be the heart-and-center of the United States's European policy, for the survival of a unified Germany is as dependent on the support of the United States as the survival of the Federal Republic has been.

It will be a task fraught with daunting problems: the Russian Army still stands on German soil; the wreckage left behind by communist mismanagement still litters the road to that equality in economic prosperity that political unification promised. The transfer of capital from West to East has been lavish, and yet the impatience of the newcomers to the open market increases, for a screen no longer blurs the penurious East's view of life as it is lived in the opulent West.

In all great and unprecedented undertakings, the assumption is that things will go right. The unification of Germany, and the Westernization of East Germany, is the boldest gamble in the history of German democracy. If all does not go right, failure would activate forces that are now contained by "Americanization." These forces are not mysterious:

Germany is the geopolitical center and economic powerhouse of Europe.

Germany is the neighbor and principal trading partner of Russia.

Germany is the principal exporter to Russia of technological goods and ideas.

Germany is Russia's bridge to Europe's democratic societies.

Where Germany goes, there goes Russia.

This does not mean that where Russia goes there goes Germany. In history, Germany never has. But the pull of one on the other has been enormous. Herr Genscher made his career as Germany's most durable statesman by telling not only his countrymen but also their allies how strong it is.[3] It would be an ironic tragedy of immense proportions if, West Germany having absorbed East Germany, the united nation turned its face eastward.

Notes

1. Konrad Adenauer (1876-1967) was the first chancellor of the Federal Republic of Germany (1949-1963). "A Christian Democrat and firmly anti-Communist, he supported NATO, and he worked to reconcile Germany with its former enemies, especially France.... During Adenauer's chancellorship his opponents had demanded that Germany be neutralized and placed in a position of nonalignment between the Eastern and Western blocs. But Adenauer and his party won all major elections because they declared that the risks to security in such a policy would be intolerable." *The New Encyclopaedia Britanica*, s.v. "Adenauer."

   Robert Schuman (1886-1963), a member of the Franch Résistance and a founder of the Roman Catholic Mouvement Républicain Populaire, served as France's minister of finance (1946), premier (1947-48), foreign minister (1948-1952), and minister of justice (1955-56). As foreign minister, in 1950, he proposed the Schuman Plan to control the production of steel and coal in France and West Germany under an authority that would be open to other European countries. The proposal was realized as the European Coal and Steel Community, and became the first in a series of economic agreements leading to the European Economic Community.

2. Jean Monnet (1888-1979) was deputy secretary general of the League of Nations (1919-1923). After the liberation of France, Monnet became head of France's National Planning Board. In 1950, he helped engineer a treaty that created the European Coal and Steel Community, and from 1952 to 1955, he served as the first president of the European Coal and Steel Community's High Authority. From 1956 to 1975, he was president of the Action Committee for the United States of Europe.

3. Hans-Dietrich Genscher (b. March 21, 1927) was interior minister of the Federal Republic of Germany from 1969 to 1974, and foreign minister from 1974 to 1992. His accommodationist policies towards the Soviet Union during the cold war constituted a major breach in the solidarity that was required to make containment effective.

25

The Middle East

In the order of U.S. priorities in the Middle East, the security of Israel stands first; the secure access to the oil wells of the Gulf stands second. Today, the Soviet threat to U.S. strategic control of the Middle East has evaporated and, with it, the threat to Israel of an attack by the former Soviet Union's Muslim clients. The security of the region's oil is not quite so certain—witness the Gulf War—but under all likely constellations of power, regional or global, the U.S. strategic domination of the Middle East is absolute, and it will—as far as fallible statesmanship can foresee—remain unchallenged.

The Soviet Union, before its demise, aspired, as did a long line of Russian czars, to the status of a Middle Eastern power. Since it did not possess a territorial base in the Middle East, it sought to force its entry into the region by proxy. It backed the claims of the radical Islamic states that, though they disagreed on most issues, had in common hostility to the state of Israel. The Soviet Union supplied the costly weaponry, the military expertise and the diplomatic backing that encouraged Israel's hostile neighbors to challenge its right to existence as a sovereign state. Notwithstanding the Soviets' persistent intervention in the affairs of the Middle East, exacting a heavy toll in lives and treasure, the challenge to Israel's existence has been turned back—and turned back conclusively.

The Soviets under Gorbachev seem to have begun Russia's disengagement from the affairs of the Middle East. The Russian Republic has not evinced any intention to launch itself upon initiatives in which the Soviet Union, at the height of its power, failed.

The U.S. strategic control of the region does not signify the end of violence in the region. The Middle East is the largest repository of arms outside the past and present lands of the superpowers. The hatreds that poison Middle Eastern relationships have not been quenched. Israel has not done with the ubiquitous and ever-present threat of terrorism. But the specter of superpower confrontation, ignited by local conflict, and of an attack upon Israel by a coalition of regional states, has been laid to rest.

Consequently, the value of Israel as an "asset" to U.S. strategy in the Middle East has diminished and is likely to diminish further. But the geopolitical value of Israel in the configuration of American *national* interests, regional and global, should not—and should never have been— the principal factor in the American-Israeli equation.[1] Israel is a democracy—and, despite its imperfections—an exemplary one. It is the one and only democracy in the midst of nations that, to varying degrees, are despotically governed.

The freedoms of Israel are the most powerful ideological challenge to the Islamic world. The success of Israel's democracy cannot but evoke the forces of democracy, now latent, in the Islamic world. It is a "showcase," as was West Berlin. That is why the secular and religious despotisms, domiciled in the region, have sought to break it. If it is the transcendent purpose of U.S. foreign policy to "make the world safe for democracy," then the security and well-being of democratic Israel is a priority of American foreign policy second to none. It is a moral priority; it is not contingent on strategic calculations. Nor should demographic considerations be the ultimate determinant of the American-Israeli relationship.

Here and now, the fortunes of Jewish migration worldwide are intertwined with the geopolitics of the Middle East. The pressures on Israel of immigration from the lands of the former Soviet Union are enormous. Israel is a small country wedged between Arabia and the Mediterranean Sea. It is poor in all resources except the peerless ingenuity and industry of its people. Israel might succeed—as she has succeeded before—to absorb hundreds of thousands of immigrants from European Russia and the former members of the Soviet Union. She will, as she has pledged herself to do, receive hundreds of thousands more, should the recrudescence of anti-Semitism threaten to extinguish the hard won tolerance of the peoples that, only a few years ago, gained their own freedom from notoriously intolerant regimes.

But, the question needs now to be asked: can Israel redeem its pledge to all the Jewish people still under foreign rule at a cost that it can bear?

Is there no alternative to an effort that might strain its resources to the breaking point and mortgage her future as the leading nation of the Middle East?

The alternative solution cannot be found in the Middle East. Israel has done her part in providing a haven for those of her people in the diaspora who, for whatever might be their reasons, wish to find a new home. The solution lies with the powerful and rich democracies that profess to stand for the equality of all men and abhor discrimination.

The first step that needs to be taken towards the solution of Israel's demographic problem is a fundamental revision of U.S. immigration policy, lest the issue of Jewish immigration from the former Soviet states turns unmanageable and malignant. There is enough room in America to settle all Jewish immigrants from Russia and beyond. Proceeding from that fact, appropriate changes should be made in U.S. laws governing immigration so that the Jewish population of the former USSR would have an American safety net should Russian democracy and, with it, popular tolerance succumb to their many and powerful enemies. Knowing such a safety net was in place, and guaranteed by a superpower, would persuade many Jews to take a chance on Russia, rather than flee now to Israel or the United States.

Such a reduction of the pressures on Israel, by guaranteed and virtually unlimited immigration to the United States, will strengthen rather than weaken the ties that bind America to Israel.

Israel and the United States have many common interests; many of their interests run parallel. If only by virtue of their respective location, some of their interests do not run parallel. Some conflict. But one interest they share indubitably is to defend and advance democracy. It follows that the security of Israel is a permanent concern of U.S. foreign policy.

Because of the confusion of ideological with strategic concerns, the U.S.-Israeli connection needs to be relieved of unnecessary encumbrance and the loose ends reduced to order. A formal treaty of defense—an attack on one contracting party is an attack upon the other—should formalize the U.S. implicit guarantee of Israeli security. Good diplomacy is orderly and specific.

There is no quick and easy solution to the demographic problem of Israel nor to the problem of Jewish migration worldwide. I have argued here that the two problems are separate and should be dealt with separately.

Israel being a Middle Eastern state, the demographic problem cannot be solved by the intervention, however well-meaning, of extra-regional powers, however friendly. It is Israel's sovereign prerogative to decide whom it will admit, and to decide where on its sovereign territory those it admits will settle.

The other problem is: where will Jewish emigrants from Russia and her neighbors wish to go? Some will wish to go to Israel. But some will wish to go to America. It should be U.S. policy to grant the wish of the latter without reservation, and to revise U.S. laws now governing immigration to this end. Such a liberalization of the system now in force will be fraught with difficulties. It would brave deeply rooted popular attitudes and powerful interests. Yet, there is no other alternative, for at stake is not only a viable Middle Eastern order but also the concord of the American people, multi-ethnic, multi-religious and wonderfully tolerant of the idiosyncrasies of the many parts that make up the whole of American democracy.

The Statue of Liberty—Mother of Exiles—still stands across from the tip of Manhattan, and its message, set in granite, assures the world that America will keep her door open:

> Give me your tired, your poor,
> Your huddled masses yearning to breathe free,
> The wretched refuse of your teeming shore.
> Send these, the homeless, tempest-tost to me,
> I lift my lamp beside the golden door!

I cannot think of better guidance for the foreign and domestic policies of the United States.

Notes

1. There exists a "Memorandum of Understanding between the Government of the United States and the Government of Israel on Strategic Cooperation," signed on November 30, 1981. According to the Preamble, "This memorandum... builds on the mutual security relationship that exists between the two nations." According to Article I, Section B, it exists "to provide each other with military assistance for operations of their forces in the area that may be required." See Karen L. Puschel, *U.S.-Israeli Strategic Cooperation in the Post–Cold War Era: An American Perspective* (Boulder, Colo.: Westview Press, 1992).

26

India, China, and the
Demographic Revolution

At the last count, 890 million Indians live side by side with 1.2 billion Chinese who, at present rates of procreation, will have risen, before the end of this century, by another 150 and 125 million, respectively, to a combined total of 2.4 billion.[1] Of course, these rough calculations—no reliable count having been taken recently in either country—are premised on the assumption that present political boundaries of India and China will indefinitely remain the same, that demographical policies will remain the same, and that mankind will be spared a genocidal war.

Where would the Indian, where would the Chinese go, if he were unable to survive at home, and were allowed to leave? He might want to go where his Kith and Kin have gone, namely, the highly developed Rimlands of the Pacific that attract foreign capital and labor. But the numbers involved would be relatively small, and even these would be contingent on the continuity of the industrial boom that has revolutionized the economies of Singapore, Malaysia, Thailand, and Indonesia. Nor could emigration of a few thousands of Indians and Chinese to the West—Western Europe and South/Central America—relieve population pressure calculated in millions.

Logically, it is the great empty spaces of Asian Russia that beckon mass emigration. That is where the emigrant should find, to his advantage and Russia's profit, a new home. Unfortunately, for both Chinese and Russians, strategic considerations and xenophobic nationalism preclude a rational solution to this problem in human geography.

(There is, however, an alternative to the relaxation of population pressure by mass migration. The most densely populated states in Europe are, per capita, the richest. Belgium, Holland, and Switzerland have, by dint of technological and financial capabilities, managerial skills, and political sophistication, succeeded in turning density of population into their most valuable economic asset—and in keeping their populations at home. They are model democracies, with political idiosyncrasies to which their institutions allow full play.)

The problem that the demographic revolution poses for mankind has lately been shunted aside. Because the cold war aggravated so many ills that have, for centuries, plagued the system of sovereign nations states, its end has been hailed by all the democratic governments and all the free media of communication as a giant step towards a secure world order at peace. Self-delusion and hypocrisy are well met: the menace to humanity of genocidal rage armed with nuclear weapons is the overarching reality of world politics and will haunt mankind as long as the demographic revolution proceeds to unhinge all international relationships.

The gut appeal of Hitler's National Socialism was its promise of more "living space" for crowded Germany. In the event, he murdered—with now obsolete lethal devices—many millions of people, thus making available additional living space to crowded Germany. Had he won the war he started, he would undoubtedly have applied this method of demographic adjustment to all the lands he conquered. What would he have done if he had possessed himself of nuclear weapons? The question is not a rhetorical one. For the West, history—the history of concord and conflict between Western states—seems to have ended. But for Asia, history—the history of the global demographic revolution—is about to begin. What will despotic rulers of poor and densely populated lands do if they possess nuclear weapons and need not fear nuclear retaliation to their nuclear gambit? This question, too, is a hard one, calling for a hard answer. So far, the answer of democratic statesmanship has been muffled by its reluctance to squash the public's high hopes engendered by the end of the cold war. Sufficient unto the day is the evil thereof.

India

The most important fact about India is India's commitment to democracy. Aristotle held that a state needs to be small in order to keep democracy alive. India, the most populous democracy in history, refutes him. The American democracy started small; it is now, next to India, the biggest. The hugeness of India's population and the multiplicity of languages and religious beliefs have militated against a smooth transition from colonial dependency to popular sovereignty. Indian democracy has survived the susceptibility of its intellectual elite to Marxist ideology.

Aside from the hugeness of their respective population and territory, India and China do not resemble one another. The response of the Chinese state to the dissent of its people from the official ideology has been massive repression. The foreign policy of China has been expansionist. The territorial gains of communist China obtained by force (Tibet and Manchuria) have been larger than those of any expansionist power active during the reign of the United Nations. China is a prime exporter of technologies of mass destruction. Certainly, China's political institutions cannot be mistaken for those of a democratic state, and the future prospect of democracy in China is dim.

India is a federal republic, multi-ethnic, multi-lingual. Her government issues from the direct suffrage of all the people. The Indian people cherish their democratic institutions. The succession of duly elected governments in New Delhi has been unbroken. The assumption by the federal government of executive power in some of the states has been brief. In the event, these measures were prompted by emergencies with which state governments could not deal. They did not exceed the constitutional limits of federal authority.

Indian democracy survived under the pressure of catastrophic events that would have tested the stamina of the seasoned democracies of the West. The resiliency of Indian democracy is, in part, due to the Indian people's affinity for those values and mores that, as Tocqueville saw it, predispose a people to democracy, but, also to the fact that India's elites have, for two centuries, spoken and read English, the language of John Locke, Adam Smith, and John Stuart Mill.

The bequest to India of British colonialism has not been—as charged by its critics, most of whom are English speakers—the corruption of its ancient culture and a gnawing inferiority complex but the infrastructure of a modern democratic state. That is what the best of her British masters wanted India to be. By the evidence, pro and contra, accumulated during the last forty years, they have not failed altogether.

American foreign policy has not yet allotted India a place among its priorities, commensurate with India's material and spiritual resources and commitment to freedom in diversity. It is this pledge to democracy that American diplomacy avows to have been the precondition of Russia's access to the bounties of the free, the open world market—and which, so far, China has staunchly withheld.

Why should this be? What counts for more: the primacy of democratic values or the calculus of strategic and economic gains? In the case of China, it has been the latter that has carried the day in the making of U.S. foreign policy. But I have argued in these pages that the purpose of American foreign policy is, and cannot help being, the advancement of democracy throughout the world—to "make the world safe for democracy," Woodrow Wilson having been ahead of his time by sixty years. I have also argued that this is the one and only foreign policy that, at the end of day, will win the support of the American people, notwithstanding their isolationist bent, and that, hence, the Wilsonian idealism of the 1920s is the realism of the 1990s.

The real issues of international politics allow for no other alternative. Only democracy can assure the openness of information about weapons of mass destruction that is the *sine qua non* of global, *real* disarmament. Democracies, dedicated to leisure and consumption, abhor the deprivations that war imposes on the populace. Therefore, they will not war upon each other, nor, on the downside, rally, in good time, their collective forces in defense of a world order under freedom, peace, and justice.

As a matter of principle, the United States should stand by its fellow democracy, India, and, if China were to persist in its expansionist pressures upon India, to contain Chinese imperialism—as it has contained Soviet imperialism. Here, the choice before U.S. foreign policy is between ideological consistency and geopolitical pragmatism, between the solidarity of all democratic peoples and the exigencies of the balance of power politics overriding all other considerations; between morality and expediency. United States diplomacy has no stronger card to play in its bid for the leadership of democracy worldwide than the rapprochement with India.

India is the only Asian power with the weight that, on the scale of power, could balance the weight of China. At present, India does not incline to play that role. As a matter of fact, it would vehemently reject the offer, if it were made by the only power that could make it, namely the United States. Yet, the collapse of the Soviet Union and the dynamics of Chinese imperialism leave India no other alternative but to realign its foreign policies.

India's rulers are not nuclear innocents. With Soviet help, India has entered the clandestine class of nuclear-capable nations, an unavowed distinction it now shares with at least a dozen nations other than the permanent members of the U.N. Security Council, who are allowed to rank officially as nuclear powers by the dint of their status as acknowledged great powers.

India has been unresponsive to the pressures of American arms-control diplomacy. It has argued that its unilateral agreement to arms reductions and nuclear nonproliferation, or an agreement of the South Asian governments to abstain from nuclear armament in perpetuity, would not reduce or abolish the nuclear capabilities of China. The argument is hard to refute. India's neighbor, along a frontier of 1,194 miles, is a police state of 1,250 million people, unfettered by any meaningful agreement on arms control.

China

The American public accepted President Richard Nixon's 180-degree turnaround towards the Maoist regime with surprising equanimity and not so surprising cynicism. The first step in understanding American foreign policy towards China is to recall why the president's policy was popular.

In 1972, the just but disastrous war in Vietnam had threatened to divide not only the American people but also the Atlantic Alliance. Europe's skepticism, discreet at first, about the wisdom of diverting American energies from the principal theater of East-West confrontation to a former European colony on the periphery of Asia had turned into open and clamorous criticism of the U.S. foreign policies the world over. The time had come to check the Soviets' probes for the soft spots in the U.S. strategy of containment. American popular opinion agreed, displaying a sophistication about the gap between the principles and the praxis of U.S. foreign policy.

President Nixon's brilliant diplomacy in 1972 tilted the balance of power against the Soviet Union. The Kremlin scratched whatever notions it might have entertained about exploiting the Vietnam debacle. In this, the most perilous moment of post-World War II history, President Nixon's bold improvisation righted the balance of power and restored the initiative to American diplomacy.

That did not mean, however, that Americans' detestation of Maoist despotism had grown soft—as soft as the eminences in academia and business, who professed to see in China's diplomatic tilt to America a mellowing of ideological orthodoxy and popular xenophobia. The octogenarians were remarkably adroit at briefly opening doors to tourism and trade, and then slamming them shut with a bang upon the slightest sign of internal reformist ardor.

Since then, twenty years of history have rolled by, most of it unanticipated by even the most farseeing statesmen. China is no longer the same makeweight in the global balance of power that President Nixon deemed essential to righting it. No longer is the Chinese factor needed to offset the Soviet factor, the latter having been removed altogether from the equation.

Although the great revaluation of all values, now taking place wherever foreign policy is made, puts in doubt the "value" of China in the U.S. balance-of-power diplomacy, it does not signify the isolation of China in world politics. Quite to the contrary, the dissolution of China's de facto alliance with the United States against the Soviet Union has freed Chinese foreign policy from the restraints implicit in that tactical conciliation of irreconcilable strategic interests. Now, there is no longer any consideration of U.S. interests that restrains China's quest for hegemony in the Third World—except, as before the rapprochement crafted by President Nixon, the power of the United States. Almost unnoticed by the foreign policy community and masked by the efflorescence of U.S.-Chinese trade, the U.S.-Chinese relationship has returned to the confrontational status quo ante. Beijing is unresponsive to American sensibilities about the trade in weapons of mass destruction. It does not allow American notions of arms control to interfere with the export of these very weapons made in China to countries notorious for their evasions of the international rules of nuclear nonproliferation.

A much-cited exception, good behavior in the United Nations (the Chinese did not block the U.S. quest for the Security Council's unanimous endorsement of its intervention in Iraq) cost China nothing and eased China's admission to the international trading community, and, hence, the reorganization of China's economy. Ideologically, its octogenarian rulers did not give one inch and, when pressed too hard by their democratic partners in trade, turned nasty.

Despite this, the counsel of corporate interests have prevailed over a medley of organizations dedicated to defending human rights and advocating the impositions of sanctions on China for its flagrant repression of civic dissent. Notwithstanding the protests of the latter, successive administrations have acceded to China's request for the grant of Most Favored Nation status in American foreign trade. The expectation of its friends, highly placed in industry and finance, of access to China's vast (potential) energy resources, and to the world's largest (potential) market, proved more persuasive to American politicians than the appeals of the diverse and divided opposition, which pleaded for strict observance of human rights.

Irrespective of China's compliance or noncompliance with the precepts of liberal democracy, the demographic colossus will inexorably advance upon the world. Democracy, it is said, thrives on free trade and free enterprise. The invisible hand of the market leads mankind into the promised land of democratic freedom. Indeed, capitalism has been immensely successful in bringing that about. But the directions and manner of China's progress are as unpredictable as the moves of Chinese diplomacy have always been. The score for predictive accuracy by the West's China watchers has been even worse than the record of Western futurology seeking to read the West's future from the sediments of its history. One development is predictable, for it merely extrapolates the present: the question, how to deal with China, will move to the highest rung on the ladder of U.S. priorities in world politics.

Conceivably, the calculus of strategic and of economic advantages derived from appeasing Chinese despotism might be wrong. Conceivably, a U.S.-China policy consistent with the principles of American democracy might be right on both grounds, ideological *and* strategic.

Notes

1. China: population: 1,165,888,000 (1992); growth rate: 1.3 percent; population projection for 2000: 1,291,894,000. Increase: 126,006,000. India: population: 889,700,000; growth rate: 2.03 percent; projection for 2000: 1,041,543,000. Increase: 151,843,000. *Encyclopaedia Britanica,* s.v. "China"; "India."

Part V

27

Towards a Union of the Democracies

The diplomacy of democratic states seeks to achieve its purpose by negotiation and, when an advantageous deal can be cut without recourse to arms, by compromise. That is what diplomacy is all about. In this respect, the diplomacy of democracy does not differ from the diplomacy of nondemocratic states.

It does differ, however, on one fundamental that does not weigh on the diplomacy of states not ruled by popular sovereignty: it cannot compromise the solidarity of the democratic peoples. That solidarity is, as I have tried to show in these pages, indivisible. An attack against any democratic people is an attack against all.

This fact was vaguely apprehended by the American people after World War I, stated implicitly by U.S. foreign policy in its progression towards World War II, and stated explicitly, though with reservations, in the Charter of the Atlantic Alliance. Since then, the momentum of global demographical and technological revolutions has been carrying U.S. foreign policy towards its predestined goal: the union of all democracies.

U.S. statesmanship has been reluctant to make this goal explicit. As a result, American public opinion fails to grasp the ineluctable necessity of it. And, of course, the mythology of the United Nations befogs the reality of a world at the brink of anarchy.

But such evasions do not divert the thrust of history one inch. They merely postpone but do not cancel out the meeting of the American people with the realities of a world order. It is as if the world were now holding its breath, waiting for the world's greatest federation to take the lead in transcending the system of nation-states, which no longer can meet the challenges of the postindustrial age.

Logically, the case for the political union of the democracies is irrefutable, but the path is littered with contradictions. Isolationist in its core, and abhorring the sacrifices exacted by the uses of its power in international politics, the United States is driven by both ideological and strategic imperatives to labor for the union of all democracies.

Consequently, the time has come for levelling with the country and the world, and to state, in language understandable to all, the purpose and requirements of American foreign policy. Now less than ever can American democracy tolerate a world half free and half unfree. To abdicate from its mission as the federating power of democracy would be not only a colossal strategic blunder but also a betrayal of the ideals that led American democracy from a remote corner of the globe to the heights of world power.

In these pages, I have argued that consistency equals credibility; that credibility is American diplomacy's ultimate weapon in the ceaseless struggle for the minds and hearts of all peoples, free and unfree; and that a foreign policy inconsistent with the principles of democracy is both a philosophical lapse and a strategic blunder.

It is a strategic blunder because the survival of American democracy is inextricably linked to the political and military security of all the world's democracies, great and small, none of which can alone defend itself against the forces of anarchy and despotism. Democratic idealism equals geopolitical realism. That much we can learn from recent history. Democratic idealism enlivened the West's highly realist strategy of "containment."

The relevancy to these issues of federalism—the classic federalism of the Founders enriched by the experience of scores of new nations—is so obvious as to make us wonder how the statesmen of today could miss it. One need only ask: what is it that makes the United States so compellingly attractive to world's peoples, a political and economic model—despite the fact that the governing elites of most countries profess to disdain us?

The answer is quite simple: the United States has developed and perfected a political system that checks authority with authority—and leaves each, be it the executive or the legislature or the courts, be it government or the country's innumerable private associations, be it organizations or simply the average citizen—to do what they can do best. The workings of the system do not always function so as to satisfy the criteria of perfect democracy. But here and now, the dispersion of power to semi-independent centers is philosophically the wisest, and operationally the most effective, government in place. With the least commotion and fanfare, this system has insured the fabulous prosperity and the high degree of civic contentment of our people.[1]

These insights of federalism have been applied by Americans to their foreign policy, with great success. Indeed, the federal idea has been, in this century, America's only seminal contribution to its foreign policy. Its two applications, the Marshall Plan and the North Atlantic Treaty Organization, were attenuated versions of an Atlantic Union, and, in concert, saved the free world from sharing the lot of those peoples that fell under communist despotism.

But NATO stopped far short of integrating its members politically. To everyone's surprise, the United States did not bring its considerable leverage to bear on the side of federalism and against the nation-state system.

In the first years after World War II, the people of the West would have followed the United States into virtually any experiment in community building. They had no choice but to take their cue from that one great power that had emerged undamaged from the war. But the United States let it be known that, while it welcomed supranational unions such as the European Community and West European Union, it did so only if the United States itself need not become part of them, or otherwise yield one iota of its sovereignty. This, perhaps, was the most grievous error of U.S. foreign policy after World War II: its failure to move the West towards federal unity, the unity Washington hailed in the abstract but rejected in fact.

Today, history invites us again to the drawing board. We hear on all sides that a New World Order is taking shape, one that requires a new philosophy and a new will born of that philosophy. We shall certainly require a new will, but I suggest that the requisite philosophy is already waiting for us, ready to be translated into a program of action.

It is the philosophy embodied in our own rich tradition of federalist thought, from *The Federalist Papers* to the works of Clarence Streit.[2] The first and most urgent step, therefore, is to undertake a grand review of the American federal experience; the second step is to apply the findings of that review to the conduct of America's foreign policy.

I have no doubts about the lessons to be drawn from such a review or our ability to apply them. At the end of the twentieth century, the United States has, once more, the chance to sublimate a wartime alliance into a confederal and then—*Deo volente*—a federal state. This time, we and our fellow democracies must not settle for less.

Notes

1. Tocqueville said, "No one can be more inclined than I am to appreciate the advantages of the federal system, which I hold to be one of the combinations most favorable to the prosperity and freedom of man." Alexis de Tocqueville, *Democracy in America,* vol. 1, ed. Phillips Bradley (New York: Vintage Books, 1945), p. 178. But he worried about the ability of a federal state to hold its own militarily against a national state.
2. *The Federalist Papers* nos. 15-20 are particularly relevant. Nos. 15-17 by Alexander Hamilton argue that the system established by the Articles of Confederation is crippled by multiple sovereigns; nos. 18-20 by James Madison argue that the system resembles unsuccessful leagues of the past. See also, Clarence K. Streit, *Union Now: A Proposal for a Federal Union of the Leading Democracies* (New York: Harper and Brothers Publishers, 1939); and Clarence K. Streit, *Freedom's Frontier: Atlantic Union Now* (New York: Harper and Brothers Publishers, 1940).

Postscript

Democracy and Statesmanship

At the conclusion of the first volume of *Democracy in America*, Alexis de Tocqueville wrote as follows:

> There are at the present time two great nations in the world, which started from different points, but seem to tend towards the same end. I allude to the Russians and the Americans. Both of them have grown up unnoticed; and whilst the attention of mankind was directed elsewhere, they have suddenly placed themselves in the front rank among the nations, and the world learned their existence and their greatness at almost the same time.

> All other nations seem to have nearly reached their natural limits, and they have only to maintain their power; but these are still in the act of growth.... The American struggles against the obstacles which nature opposes to him; the adversaries of the Russian are men. The former combats the wilderness and savage life; the latter, civilization with all its arms. The conquests of the American are therefore gained by the ploughshare; those of the Russian by the sword. The Anglo-American relies upon personal interest to accomplish his ends, and gives free scope to the unguided strength and common sense of the people; the Russian centers all the authority of society in a single arm. The principal instrument of the former is freedom; of the latter, servitude. Their starting-point is different, and their courses are not the same; yet each of them seems marked out by the will of Heaven to sway the destinies of half the globe.[1]

In this century, of course, Tocqueville's prediction came true—the global forces of autocracy, led first by Germany but then by Russia, confronted the global forces of democracy, led first by Britain but then by the United States.

To say this, however, tells us only two things: what the course of that protean ideological confrontation has been to date, and what the strategy of America must be hereafter.

We know that, after years of anguished passivity, the democratic peoples rallied, first against Germany, then against the Soviet Union. The despots were defeated, though much precious time had been frittered away in tedious debate before democracy prevailed. All too long the despots were allowed to roam the world and spread their evil message. All too many lives were lost that prompt precautionary action could have saved. Democracy's pace in foreign policy may be sure, but unquestionably it tends to be slow—as slow as the bureaucratic procedures of the welfare state, as slow as decision making by popular participation.

As for the future strategy of America, that too is clear: the foreign policy of the United States *is* democracy. The United States makes democracy the measure of its engagements in international politics. It makes a state's commitment to democratic ideals the measure of its own commitment to that state's military security and economic prosperity. Its goal is indeed to "make the world safe for democracy."[2] In fact, as long as American democracy remains alive in the hearts and minds of the American people, America cannot have any other foreign policy.

The crucial, the fateful, question is whether the American people have the will to bear the burden of the one and only foreign policy that serves the cause of freedom at home by advancing the cause of freedom everywhere. The costs of that policy will be enormous—as enormous as the costs to America of victory in World War II, the economic restoration of a democratic Europe, and victory in the cold war.

The argument that the American democracy can no longer afford the cost of global leadership is both feckless and wrong. The argument that the survival of democracy at home calls for the withdrawal of American power from present and future commitments to the defense of freedom abroad is not only odious but irrational. While the United States fought this century's great wars, hot and cold, its gross national product and median standard of living increased spectacularly—so spectacularly as to set the example, worldwide, of peaceful economic development. The United States grew richer as it grew more powerful, and grew more powerful as it grew richer. This is a fact—proved by overwhelming statistical evidence.

Why, then, these counsels of defeatism, of abdication from world leadership, at the very moment when the profound alterations of the international balance of power call for American leadership and open unprecedented opportunities for it?

Among the several "weaknesses" of democracy in America to which Tocqueville addressed the concluding chapters of his book, he notes one that affects the conduct of a democracy's foreign policy more adversely than any other: "The difficulty that a democracy finds in conquering the passions and subduing the desires of the moment with a view to the future is observable in the United States in the most trivial things."[3]

Virtually all important foreign policies are long range. That is why foreign policy needs, above all other attributes, consistency. Statesmanship that is not consistent is a contradiction in terms. Foreign policy making that is not guided by a "view of the future" is blind. Yet, the great mass of the people are driven by "immediate needs."

Even in domestic politics, a grand "view of the future" brings out the vote of only a minority that has the time and intellectual detachment to meditate on issues of general interest. But that holds true with a vengeance for the issues of world politics, which are remote from the average voter's experience; which call for vast expenditures barren of assured returns; and which seem contingent on the behavior, good or bad, of foreign peoples.

Hence the volatility of foreign policy's constituency. Hence also the over-arching need for a "view of the future" that rouses the hearts and the minds of the American people to the primacy of foreign policy over all policies.

Of course, it is the axiom of isolationist politics that, today, a "view of the future" is not needed, for the American public is so well informed about foreign affairs that it can react instantly and pragmatically to events of the moment, dispensing with a view of the world's future. After all, does not technological progress in the means of communication allow the public to watch international politics as it is being made: in the meetings of foreign ministers, in the conclaves of the United Nations, in the clashes of factions in parliamentary debate, in the street, in the armed contests between incumbent governments and rebels, in the confrontations of the forces of order and terrorism, and in wars between states—and all this live and in color? What need, then, for principles, consistency, and long-range policies?

The trouble with this claim is not that it is altogether false, but that it is based on half-truths—as are all claims made on behalf of the social and moral betterment that allegedly accrues to mankind from technological progress. Technology is neutral, socially and morally. The two natures of technology—the one creative and the other destructive—

should, by now, be as plain to all peoples, developed or developing, as the rising and setting of the sun.

Information is indeed the life line of democracy—as long as there is plenty of it and no one is allowed to edit it too closely before it flows to the consumer. The cardinal assumption of popular government remains what it has always been: that the people can eventually distinguish truth from falsity, as long as the media supplies them with "all the news fit to print." At the end of the day, the people in their wisdom will sift the truth from the stream of information, mostly muddy, about domestic and foreign politics. Such is the mighty assumption of democracy.

But if the media, at their best, can help us to learn, with considerable accuracy, where we have been and where we are, no one should expect the media to tell us where we are going—or where we ought to go. That is the job of the statesman: foresight is the mark of his calling. His is the task to persuade the people to "silence their immediate needs with a view of the future." The history of democratic foreign policy is the history of men who succeeded or failed at this task.

Notes

1. Alexis de Tocqueville, *Democracy in America,* vol. 1, ed. Phillips Bradley (New York: Vintage Books, 1945), p. 452.
2. The exact words of President Woodrow Wilson were: "The world must be made safe for democracy." The occasion was a speech to Congress on April 2, 1917.
3. Tocqueville, *Democracy in America,* vol. 1, p. 238.

Index